Bibliography on World Conflict and Peace

Other Titles in This Series

Conflict Resolution, Paul Wehr

The Myth of Victory: What Is Victory in War? Richard W. Hobbs

Westview Special Studies in Peace, Conflict, and Conflict Resolution

Bibliography on
World Conflict and Peace: Second Edition
compiled by Elise Boulding, J. Robert Passmore,
and Robert Scott Gassler

The authors present more than 1,000 entries organized in twenty-six major categories in the fields of conflict and peace studies; they also list relevant bibliographies, abstracts, collections, annuals, series, and periodicals. Though the emphasis is on global systems, the structures and processes of conflict and peacemaking are covered as they apply at every level from interpersonal to international. This is the first book of its kind to take equal account of the needs of teachers, students, researchers, activists, journalists, practitioners, and policymakers. Material is drawn from the diciplines of sociology, political science, economics, anthropology, geography, history, psychology, and the humanities.

Elise Boulding, professor of sociology at the University of Colorado, is currently Montgomery Visiting Professor in the Department of Sociology at Dartmouth College. She is on the editorial board of *Peace and Change: A Journal of Peace Research*, is a member of the U.S. National Commission for UNESCO, and is on the board of directors of the Institute for World Order.

J. Robert Passmore is doing graduate work in sociology at the University of Colorado.

Robert Scott Gassler holds an M.S. in library science; he is now in the Ph.D. program in economics at the University of Colorado.

Published in cooperation with
the Consortium on Peace Research,
and the Section on the Sociology
of World Conflicts of the
American Sociological Association

Bibliography on World Conflict and Peace: Second Edition

compiled by Elise Boulding,
J. Robert Passmore, and
Robert Scott Gassler

Westview Press / Boulder, Colorado

Westview Special Studies in Peace, Conflict, and Conflict Resolution

Published in 1979 in the United States of America by
Westview Press, Inc.
5500 Central Avenue
Boulder, Colorado 80301
Frederick A. Praeger, Publisher

Library of Congress Catalog Number: 79-467
ISBN: 0-89158-374-2

Composition for this book was provided by the author.
Printed and bound in the United States of America.

Contents

Acknowledgments

Many people have contributed their knowledge and perspectives to the compilation of this bibliography, not least the many faculty and students in peace studies programs around the country who have used and commented on it. This present revised edition has been greatly aided by the critique and suggestions of two economists, Kenneth Boulding and Emile Benoit, who went over it shortly before he died. The suggestions of political scientists Chadwick Alger, Manus Midlarsky, Francis Beer, and J. David Singer have been highly valued. The manuscript had the benefit of critique by sociologists Louis Kriesberg and Paul Wehr and from peace studies specialists Hanna Newcombe of the Canadian Peace Research Institute, Betty Reardon of the Institute of World Order, and Susan Carpenter, formerly with the Future Studies Program of the University of Massachusetts at Amherst. Suggestions were also made by active COPRED members Neil H. Katz, Cheryl Hoffman Keene, Warren F. Kuehl, Patricia Mische, Burns Weston, and Lillian Genser.

J. Robert Passmore, a graduate student at the University of Colorado, and I coauthored the original bibliography. Bob has developed the bibliographic skills required for such a project in the peace studies context over a period of nearly eight years, with the advice of scholars associated with the developing world conflicts group in the American Sociological Association and with the Committee on Research Utilization of the Consortium on Peace Research, Education and Development (COPRED). Edward Azar as Chair of that Committee advised in the early stages of the project. Scott Gassler, a graduate student in economics and a specialist in library science, joined us in the preparation of the revised bibliography and contributed greatly to the revised classification system. In addition, Girma Negash, a political science graduate student from Ethiopia, worked closely with us in developing the classification system, in adding to the main listing and especially the periodicals section, and in generally adding a Third World perspective to the project. We feel that this close collaboration of two sociologists, a political scientist and an economist in developing the revised bibliography has made it more representative of the interdisciplinary field of conflict and peace studies than the original bibliography was. Nancy Wood and Dick Williams, graduate students associated with the Conflict and Peace Studies Program at the University of Colorado, have also worked on it, as have undergraduate students from that program, in particular Bill Ferrell (first edition) and Sylvia Labrucherie (second edition).

The Program of Research in General Social and Economic Dynamics of the Institute of Behavioral Science at the University of Colorado, under the direction of Kenneth Boulding, has been very supportive of the bibliography project from its earliest beginnings. Without the intellectual, moral and financial support of that program the bibliography would never have been possible. We are all grateful to Kenneth Boulding, and to his administrative assistant, Vivian Wilson. Another indispensable person for this project has been Dorothy Carson, my administrative assistant, who also worked on the project from its very beginning. She played many roles, from editor to layout person to typist to publisher and distributor of the first edition. Judy Fukuhara was the skilled and patient typist who produced the final copy of the first and second editions. Jacqueline Myers also assisted by typing the first draft of the second edition. The bibliography has been a collective enterprise in the best sense of the word. For me personally, it has been a great privilege to work with so many wise and responsive collaborators from the North American conflict and peace studies community in the preparation of this work.

E. B.

Introduction

Originally a joint product of the Consortium on Peace Research, Education and Development (COPRED) and the American Sociological Association's Committee on the Sociology of World Conflicts (now the Section on the Sociology of World Conflicts), this bibliography was first compiled as a mimeographed booklet primarily in response to the needs of teachers and students in the new field of conflict and peace studies. It was also intended for the use of researchers, practitioners in the field of conflict management, and lay persons concerned with the issues of global conflict and peacemaking.

Since there has been a steady demand for this bibliography from the day of publication by all four groups--teachers, researchers, practitioners, and concerned lay persons--the decision was made to revise and update the bibliography in consultation with various scholars in the field. This book is the product of that consultation. Like the first edition, it is intended primarily for North American use, and cannot be considered a definitive international bibliography. While the work of the international peace research community is well represented here, and international journals have been extensively utilized in preparing this bibliography, the user will nevertheless note that the majority of the books listed have been published in North America and that only the U.S. publishers are listed for those also published elsewhere. This is in part because library availability of books has been an important criterion for inclusion in the bibliography. Since the peace research community is an international community, however, international coverage is important and can in itself contribute to availability. We have therefore included

European publications we feel should be in American peace studies libraries. Since Europe is the main stronghold of the peace community, there are proportionately more European entries than entries from other parts of the world. In time, an internationally prepared bibliography of conflict and peace studies should become available.

The starting point for the original bibliography was the description of the field of conflict and peace studies as prepared by the Committee on the Sociology of World Conflicts. The Committee's definition of the field was utilized in selecting the original materials to be included. Although the statement had been prepared in terms of concepts and subject domains familiar to sociologists, all the social sciences were nevertheless drawn on in compiling the bibliography. The new revised bibliography takes more account of the perspectives of political science and, to a degree, of economics, while nevertheless retaining a sociological frame of reference. The Committee on the Sociology of World Conflicts had concluded that the following labels cover the field as it is now generally conceived:

> ...war and peace, international conflict, transnational relations, imperialism, and international relations. In other words, we are interested in large collectivities such as nation states, ethnic groups, political movements, and religions, whose conflicting relations both involve and may transcend national state boundaries. In order to comprehend such conflicts, we must also take into account the non-conflicting relations at least insofar as they affect the awareness of conflicts, how they are conducted, and what their outcomes are.[1]

Put in a more interdisciplinary framework, a description of the field might also read as follows:

> The study of those characteristics of the total world social systems which make peace more probable.

---

[1] Report of the Ad Hoc Committee on War and Peace Studies, Footnotes, American Sociological Association (August 1973), p. 16.

Peace research represents a new kind of focus on planetary social structures that cuts across all disciplinary boundaries in the social sciences. Peace researchers are therefore recruited from economics, sociology, political science, psychology, geography, history, anthropology, with increasing participation from scholars in the humanities. Using a general systems framework, they use concepts from all kinds of fields in the study of the structures and processes of conflict and peacemaking and apply them at every level from intrapersonal, psychic conflict to international conflict. They are committed to putting planetary welfare ahead of any particular national interest.[2]

Criteria for Inclusion of Items

In trying to meet the needs of a variety of potential users, we have had to make many difficult decisions about inclusion or exclusion of specific items. In general, we have used the following criteria:

1. Items should be relevant to or have implications for the understanding of world conflict and peace processes. However, the skills learned at other levels of conflict management can become relevant to the understanding of world conflicts. Thus we have not adhered strictly to the domain of research addressed to conflict outside national boundaries, including for instance works on family conflict (e.g. Bard, E. Boulding), ethology (e.g. Ardrey, Lorenz), nonviolent community action (e.g. Charny, Oppenheimer and Lakey, Shivers and Olson, Walker), and also community conflict (e.g. Coleman, Dasgupta).
2. The following categories of materials have been included:
    a) Scholarly works (theoretical, historical, and empirical), especially

[2] Elise Boulding, "American Friends and Peace Research," Friends Journal, XX, 4 (February 15, 1974), 100-103.

that of a comparative nature (e.g. Wright (1965), Fox, Singer (ed., 1968))

b) Journalistic writings which contribute significant perspectives on conflict and peace (e.g. Halberstam)

c) Advocacy writings which have made significant contributions to scholarly research and/or public discussion (e.g. Angell, Ardrey, Artin, Einstein, Melman, Reves).

d) Educational materials of direct use in classrooms at each level of education (see entries labeled EDUCATION)

3. Since the publication of major works on the theory of nonviolent social action continues (e.g. Erikson; Ganguli; Sharp (1973)), we are particularly interested in attempting to include relevant works representing the several topics under NONVIOLENCE.

4. The rise of a literature on conflict and economic growth and development has prompted our attention to the categories of DEVELOPMENT, LIBERATION, RESOURCES, and TERRORISM, representing both newly-emphasized problems and newly-described responses.

5. Other topics relevant to world conflict are major academic specializations in their own right, and thus we have been very selective in these areas. Foreign policy studies and materials from the existing fields of economics, international studies, political science, and sociology have been included only when they represent classic statements in their own field with particular significance for conflict studies or when they are of a comparative nature with theoretical implications.

6. The importance of contributions to the field by the early conflict theorists in economics, political science, and sociology has been acknowledged by their inclusion.

7. This bibliography focuses on works published from 1945 through 1978. We are pleased that the monumental task of compiling an annotated historical bibliography is nearing completion at the University of Illinois; it will make a fine complement to

the present one: Berenice A. Carroll and Clinton S. Fink. Polemology and Irenology: An Annotated Bibliography of Peace Theory and Peace Research, 1800-1945.

Some Suggestions on How to Use the Bibliography

There are four sections to the bibliography: the main listing; Collections, Annuals, and Series; Periodicals; and Bibliographies.

The main listing includes monographs, compilations, and a few articles in scholarly journals. Entries are arranged by author (or title if necessary).

Subject-category labels appear on the left margin alongside each entry. There are 26 major categories, each having several subtopics. These labels are listed and described in the Subject Guide immediately preceding the main listing. It is a good idea to study the Guide to develop an idea of the range of topics included and to determine how to find references in a given area of interest.

The user may then choose a set of subject-category labels appropriate to his or her research and then scan the labels in the main section for a list of citations. The use of key words is intended to simplify this task. All entries are listed alphabetically by author, and thus as a person becomes familiar with principal authors in a specialization, the publications of these authors may also be checked for appropriate citations. To facilitate searches by author, all second authors or editors are cross-referenced. This means that it is possible, in principle at least, to derive a list of all entries for which a person is a joint author or editor as well as principal author.

The filing order is straightforward: all listings under the same person's name are arranged alphabetically by title (even when there is more than one author or editor), followed by cross-references. Names beginning with "Mc" or "Mac" are all arranged as though spelled "Mac."

The section on Collections, Annuals, and Series includes major multivolume works, identifies some important series undertaken by publishers, and lists other serials issued annually (especially yearbooks) or irregularly. All entries are listed in alphabetical order by author, editor, or issuing group.

Periodicals (other than yearbooks) are listed in the following section in alphabetical order by title. Information on frequency of publication, editor, beginning date of publication, and publisher are provided for each journal. Subscription prices are not listed since they are likely to be out of date very soon.

The final section, Bibliographies, has been included because a number of publications on specialized topics exist. Considerable effort has been made to select references from a broad range of topics and to emphasize annotated bibliographies. These entries have again been arranged by compiler's name or issuing agency, and a brief description of the contents is provided in some cases.

Finally, while the main listing offers an introduction to the wide scope of published material on the study of world conflict and peace, the last three sections list major, more specialized works. These later sections cover topics such as foreign policy studies and international economics which the main listing deemphasizes. Thus these three sections will help readers locate important additional materials on, for example, the sociology of war, military sociology, game theory, warfare in particular geographic regions, and case studies of conflict.

Some Sources of Literature on War/Peace Studies

Since some of the materials listed in the bibliography are published by organizations which specialize in peace and conflict research--and are most readily available from them--we are furnishing below a selected list of these organizations with their addresses. Since such a list is out-of-date by the time it is published, it should be used with caution.

Canadian Peace Research Institute
Norman Z. Alcock, Director
119 Thomas Street
Oakville, Ontario
Canada

Center for the Study of Armament and Disarmament
California State University, Los Angeles
Los Angeles, California 90032

Center for War/Peace Studies
Robert W. Gilmore, President
Doris Shamleffer, Director of Resources
218 East 18th Street
New York, New York 10003

Consortium on Peace Research, Education
and Development
William Kenney, Executive Director
Bethel College
North Newton, Kansas 67117

Gandhi Peace Foundation
221-223 Deen Dayal Upadhyaya Marg,
New Delhi 110-001
India

Gandhian Institute of Studies
P.O. Box 116
Rajghat, Varanasi-221001
India

Institute for World Order
Robert Johansen, President
1140 Avenue of the Americas
New York, New York 10036

International Peace Research Association (IPRA)
IPRA Secretariat
P.O. Box 5052
Oslo 3,
Norway

Peace Science Society (International)
Department of Peace Science
3718 Locust Walk
University of Pennsylvania
Philadelphia, Pennsylvania 19174

Richardson Institute for Conflict and
Peace Research
Department of Politics
University of Lancaster
Fylde College
Bailrigg, Lancaster LA1 4YF
England

Stockholm International Peace Research
Institute (SIPRI)
Dr. Frank Barnaby, Director
Sveavägen 166
S-113 46 Stockholm
Sweden

Tampere Peace Research Institute
Tammelan puistokatu 58 B V
33100 Tampere 10
Finland

United Nations Institute for Training and
Research (UNITAR)
801 United Nations Plaza
New York, New York 10017

UNITAR
Palais des Nations
CH-1211
Geneva 10
Switzerland

Worldwatch Institute
1776 Massachusetts Avenue, N.W.
Washington, D.C. 20036

World Without War Council of the United States
Office of the President
1730 Grove Street
Berkeley, California 94709

Mention should be made of another organization;

ERIC/CHESS (Educational Resources Information
Center, Clearing House for Social Studies/
Social Science Education)
855 Broadway
Boulder, Colorado 80302

Not strictly a peace organization, it has an indexing and abstracting service (included in the monthly publication Research in Education), a research and referral service, and a computer retrieval system which contains information on subjects related to conflict and peace studies.

Our Request to Users

This bibliography will be periodically revised and updated in the future. We welcome any corrections and suggestions you may have regarding both content and style for future editions. Send all communications to: World Conflict and Peace Bibliography Project, c/o Elise Boulding, Institute of Behavioral Science, University of Colorado, Boulder, Colorado 80309.

Elise Boulding
J. Robert Passmore
Robert Scott Gassler
December 1, 1978

Subject Guide to the Bibliography on World Conflict and Peace

Aggression	See VIOLENCE
Alliances	See I. POLITICAL e
ARMS	Modern Weapons and the threat of war; Arms race; New weapons (Compare: DISARMAMENT) 1. Theory 2. History; case studies 3. Measurement; prediction 4. Political aspects 5. Social aspects 6. Economic aspects a. Deterrence studies b. Studies of specific weapons systems (e.g., ICBM's, CBW, submarines, etc.)
ATTITUDES	Attitudes, values, and ideology: including political socialization, images of war and peace, collective perceptions and attitude formation (See also CONFLICT h) 1. Theory 2. History; case studies (See also FUTURES 2) 3. Measurement; prediction 4. Political aspects 5. Social aspects a. Attitude change; propaganda, persuasion and conversion
CONFLICT	General conflict processes, social conflict. (Compare: INTEGRATION; see also MEDIATION)

1. Theory
2. History; case studies
3. Measurement; prediction
4. Political aspects
5. Social aspects
6. Economic aspects
7. Psychological and social-psychological aspects

a. Relationships between internal and external conflict
b. Conflict as gaming (See I. POLITICAL e)
c. Conflict as status discrepancy and structural violence
d. Class conflict
e. Coalition formation
f. Events analysis
g. Cross-pressure and multiple-loyalty
h. Ideological conflict

Conversion — See DISARMAMENT 6

CRISIS — Crisis behavior, development of crises

1. Theory
2. History; case studies
3. Measurement; prediction
4. Political aspects
5. Social aspects
6. Economic aspects
7. Psychological and social-psychological aspects

a. Crisis intervention (See also MEDIATION)
b. Studies on the outbreak of war or conflict
c. Studies of the termination of war and of conflict settlement (See also MEDIATION a)

DEVELOPMENT — Dependency-interdependency relationships, development, colonialism, imperialism (includes both "dependency" and "development")

1. Theory
2. History; case studies
3. Measurement; prediction
4. Political aspects
5. Social aspects
6. Economic aspects

7. Psychological and social-psychological aspects
a. Technical assistance
b. North-South relationships
c. Dependency, imperialism and colonialism (See also RESOURCES, TRANSNATIONAL c)
d. Ethics and social values as issues in dependency relationships

DISARMAMENT	Disarmament, arms control, limitations on weapons development. (Compare: ARMS) 1. Theory 2. History, case studies 3. Measurement; prediction 4. Political aspects 5. Social aspects 6. Economic aspects (including conversion from military to civilian industry) 7. Psychological and social-psychological aspects a. Arms control and limitation b. Demilitarization
EDUCATION	Education and teaching about wars, warfare, peace and peacemaking 1. Theory 2. History; case studies (of peace education) a. Peace education in formal, non-formal and life-long learning settings b. Curriculum development and outlines c. Teaching-learning methodologies d. Value-oriented education e. Peace education in a religious context f. Peace education in the home, family life
Foreign Policy	See I. POLITICAL
FUTURES	Future problems, cultural images of the future, future world order perspectives, the functions of utopia 1. Theory

	2. History; case studies (of past images of the future) 3. Measurement; prediction a. Utopian movements b. World order models (including World Order Models Project)
Gaming	See CONFLICT b, I. POLITICAL e
INTEGRATION	Integration of nations and cultures toward a world community. The study of integration processes. (See also I. POLITICAL b, TRANS-NATIONAL) 1. Theory 2. History; case studies 3. Measurement; prediction 4. Political aspects 5. Social aspects 6. Economic aspects 7. Psychological and social-psychological aspects a. Functionalism and neo-functionalism (See also I. POLITICAL d)
I. ECONOMIC	International economic relations: trade, investments and credit 1. Theory 2. History; case studies 3. Measurement; prediction 4. Political aspects 5. Social aspects a. New International Economic Order
I. LAW	International Law; relationship to world order and warfare 1. Theory 2. History; case studies 3. Social aspects a. World law proposals (e.g., World Federalism, Outlawry of War, etc.) b. Anthropological accounts of law and warfare c. Law of non-territorial spaces: the sea, space travel, planetary exploration d. Development of international legal concepts

I. ORGANIZATION	International Organizations: structure and functioning of intergovernmental organizations and agencies. (See also TRANSNATIONAL; Compare: TRANSNATIONAL) 1. Theory 2. History; case studies 3. Measurement (including measurement of network density); prediction a. Regional intergovernmental relations (See also I. POLITICAL d)
I. POLITICAL	International political relations, including diplomacy and the study of international systems 1. Theory 2. History; case studies 3. Measurement; prediction 5. Social aspects 6. Economic aspects 7. Psychological and social-psychological aspects a. National policy, decision-making of national leaders b. Alliance systems and processes c. Nation-boundary issues d. Regional relationships (See also INTEGRATION a) e. Simulation and gaming to study international politics (See also CONFLICT b) f. Studies of national power, especially "balance of power"
LIBERATION	Liberation movements: Studies of liberation, revolution, nationalism, separatism 1. Theory 2. History; case studies 3. Measurement; prediction (e.g., of "revolutionary potential") 4. Political aspects 5. Social aspects 6. Economic aspects 7. Psychological and social-psychological aspects a. Territorial and national liberation movements

b. Non-territorial and transnational liberation movements (See also TERRORISM, and WARFARE c)
c. Guerrilla warfare, both violent and non-violent

MEDIATION — Methodology and practice of conflict management and intervention to settle disputes (See also CRISIS a)
1. Theory
2. History; case studies
3. Measurement; prediction
a. Global and conflict negotiation, mediation, confrontation and settlement (See also CRISIS c)
b. Peacekeeping forces: studies and proposals regarding strategy, tactics (See also MILITARY b, CIVILIAN DEF a)

MILITARY — Military Organization: analysis of military institutions
1. Theory
2. History; case studies (includes comparative studies of military organization)
3. Measurement; prediction
4. Political aspects
5. Social aspects
6. Economic aspects
7. Psychological and social-psychological aspects
a. Nontraditional (non-military) uses of military personnel
b. Organization of peacekeeping forces (See also MEDIATION b)
c. Militarism

Movements — See LIBERATION, NONVIOLENCE, PROTEST

Multinationals — See TRANSNATIONAL 6

Negotiation — See MEDIATION a

NONVIOLENCE — Nonviolent action, strategy and ideology. Nonviolent movements and campaigns
1. Theory

	2. History; case studies 3. Measurement; prediction 4. Political aspects 5. Social aspects 6. Economic aspects (including boycotts and Gandhian economic organization) 7. Psychological and social-psychological aspects a. Advocacy of nonviolent principles, strategy b. Religious and philosophical bases of pacifism c. Socialization for nonviolence (Compare: VIOLENCE a)
Peace	See INTEGRATION, MEDIATION, NONVIOLENCE, RESEARCH
Peacekeeping	See MEDIATION b, MILITARY b
Peace movement	See PROTEST
PROTEST	Protest Movements. Collective action and social movements to protest political decisions or to generally abolish war. (Includes "war resistance" and "anti-war" movements, unique protest actions as well as worldwide peace movements) 1. Theory 2. History; case studies 4. Political aspects 5. Social aspects 6. Economic aspects 7. Psychological and social-psychological aspects a. Studies of protest actions b. Organizing for peace; peace societies c. Individual non-participation in war: non-cooperation, conscientious objection
Religion	See ATTITUDES b, NONVIOLENCE b
RESEARCH	Research on peace and war. The impact of scholarly research on peace and war, and studies of the field of peace research

a. Literature reviews, surveys of topics in the field of peace research
b. Agenda for and criticism of peace research
c. Government-sponsored research, and social science methods used in policy formation
d. Dilemmas of sponsorship of research on peace and war
e. Manuals and programs: how to do peace research

RESOURCES

Conflict over limited resources such as fuel; environmental issues generally considered in relation to world order and justice

1. Theory
2. History; case studies
4. Political aspects
6. Economic aspects

a. Global impact of environmental problems; ecological studies
b. Global impact of management of non-renewable resources
c. Human survival in the context of ecological interference and change
d. Food production and distribution

SECURITY

a. General issues of human rights
b. International responses to human rights violations
c. Perceptions of personal security
d. Public participation in policy formation
e. Collective security
f. World citizenship; transnational participation

TERRORISM

Terrorism and world order; international terrorism and social change. (See also LIBERATION c)

1. Theory
2. History; case studies
3. Measurement; prediction
4. Political aspects
5. Social aspects

a. Domestic terrorism

b. State-initiated terrorism
c. Transnational terrorism (See also LIBERATION c)
d. Strategy of terrorists
e. Counter-strategy of terrorist targets

TRANSNATIONAL — Transnational systems: global, non-governmental networks, non-governmental organizations and international associations (See also INTEGRATION 4,5,6; compare: I. ORGANIZATION)
1. Theory
2. History; case studies
3. Measurement (of organizational density, potential, etc.); prediction
4. Political aspects (including governmental support or interference)
5. Social aspects (including cultural exchange)
6. Economic aspects (including multinational business corporations)
a. Regional non-governmental relations
b. International Non-Governmental Organizations (INGO's)

VIOLENCE — Studies on violence and aggression. (See also TERRORISM)
1. Theory
2. History; case studies (including anthropological accounts)
3. Measurement; prediction
4. Political aspects
5. Social aspects
6. Economic aspects
7. Psychological and social-psychological aspects (including ethology)
a. Socialization for violence; personality, culture and violence. (Compare: NONVIOLENCE c)
b. Psycho-bioenergetic studies and animal ethology

WARFARE	Warfare as a form of social organization 1. Theory 2. History; case studies 5. Social aspects a. Total war, nuclear war, CBR warfare b. Limited war c. Revolution and guerrilla warfare (See also LIBERATION c)
Weapons	See ARMS
World Order	See FUTURES b, INTEGRATION, I. ORGANIZATION

Bibliography on World Conflict and Peace

MILITARY 5	Abercrombie, Clarence L. THE MILITARY CHAPLAIN. Beverly Hills, Calif.: Sage, 1977.
	Abramovitz, Norman, see Nesbitt, William.
EDUCATION b	Abrams, Grace, and Fran Schmidt. LEARNING PEACE: A RESOURCE UNIT. Philadelphia: Jane Addams Peace Association, 1972.
EDUCATION b	Abrams, Grace, and Fran Schmidt. SOCIAL STUDIES: PEACE IN THE TWENTIETH CENTURY. Philadelphia: Jane Addams Peace Association, 1973.
	Ackoff, Russell L., see Sisson, Roger L.
WARFARE 1	Adler, Mortimer J. HOW TO THINK ABOUT WAR AND PEACE. New York: Simon and Schuster, 1944.
ATTITUDES 1,3	Adorno, Theodore W., Else Frenkel-Brunswik, Daniel J. Levinson, and R. Nevitt Sanford. THE AUTHORITARIAN PERSONALITY. New York: Harper, 1960.

CONFLICT 1,5 RESEARCH a	Aho, James Alfred. GERMAN REALPOLITIK AND AMERICAN SOCIOLOGY. Lewisburg, Pa.: Bucknell University Press, 1975.
INTEGRATION 1,4	Ake, Claude. A THEORY OF POLITICAL INTEGRATION. Homewood, Ill.: Dorsey, 1967.
EDUCATION b I. LAW 1,2 I. ORGANIZATION 2 I. POLITICAL 1 MEDIATION 1,b RESEARCH b	Akkerman, Robert J., Peter J. van Krieken, and Charles O. Pannenborg, Editors. DECLARATIONS ON PRINCIPLES: A QUEST FOR UNIVERSAL PEACE. Leyden, The Netherlands: Sijthoff, 1977.
RESOURCES a VIOLENCE 1,5 WARFARE 1	Alcock, Norman Z. THE EMPEROR'S NEW CLOTHES. Oakville, Ontario: Canadian Peace Research Institute, 1971.
ATTITUDES 1,2 INTEGRATION 1,2,3, 5,7	Alcock, Norman Z. THE LOGIC OF LOVE. Oakville, Ontario: Canadian Peace Research Institute, 1976.
CONFLICT 1 VIOLENCE 1,5,7,a WARFARE 1	Alcock, Norman Z. THE WAR DISEASE. Oakville, Ontario: Canadian Peace Research Institute, 1977.
TERRORISM 1,2,c	Alexander, Yonah, Editor. INTERNATIONAL TERRORISM: NATIONAL, REGIONAL AND GLOBAL PERSPECTIVES. New York: Praeger, 1976.
I. ORGANIZATION 1 I. POLITICAL 1	Alger, Chadwick F. "Decision-making in the United Nations." INTERNATIONAL ASSOCIATIONS, 10 (1972), 46-465.
POLITICAL 2,3	Alger, Chadwick F. "Interaction in a Committee of the United Nations General Assembly," in J. David Singer, Editor, QUANTITATIVE INTERNATIONAL POLITICS: INSIGHTS AND EVIDENCE. New York: Free Press, 1968.

FUTURES 2 I. ORGANIZATION 2	Alger, Chadwick F. "Problems in Global Organization." INTERNATIONAL SOCIAL SCIENCE JOURNAL, 22, 4 (1970), 691-709.
POLITICAL 1	Alger, Chadwick F. "Trends in International Relations Research," in Norman D. Palmer, Editor, DESIGN FOR INTERNATIONAL RELATIONS RESEARCH: SCOPE, THEORY, METHODS, AND RELEVANCE. Philadelphia: American Academy of Political and Social Science, 1970.
	Alger, Chadwick F., see Geutzkow, Harold S.
I. ORGANIZATION 1 I. POLITICAL 1	Alker, Hayward R., Jr., and Bruce M. Russett. WORLD POLITICS IN THE GENERAL ASSEMBLY. New Haven, Conn.: Yale University Press, 1965.
	Alker, Hayward R., Jr., see Russett, Bruce M.
VIOLENCE b	Alland, Alexander. THE HUMAN IMPERATIVE. New York: Columbia University Press, 1972.
INTEGRATION 2	Allee, C. W. COOPERATION AMONG ANIMALS. New York: Schumen, 1938.
INTEGRATION 2	Allee, C. W. THE SOCIAL LIFE OF ANIMALS. New York: Schumen, 1938.
DEVELOPMENT 1,d I. ECONOMIC 4	Alvarez, Francisco Casanova. NEW HORIZONS FOR THE THIRD WORLD. Foreword by Sol M. Linowitz. Washington, D.C.: Public Affairs Press, 1976.

VIOLENCE 1,2,a	Alvik, Trond. "The Development of Views on Conflict, War, and Peace Among School Children." JOURNAL OF PEACE RESEARCH, 2 (1968), 171-195.
I. POLITICAL a	American Friends Service Committee. IN PLACE OF WAR: AN INQUIRY INTO NONVIOLENT NATIONAL DEFENSE. New York: Grossman, 1967.
TRANSNATIONAL 5	American Friends Service Committee. JOURNEY THROUGH A WALL: A QUAKER MISSION TO A DIVIDED GERMANY. Philadelphia: American Friends Service Committee, 1964.
ATTITUDES 2,a I. POLITICAL a WARFARE 2	American Friends Service Committee. SEARCH FOR PEACE IN THE MIDDLE EAST. Greenwich, Conn.: Fawcett, 1970.
ATTITUDES 1,b CIVILIAN DEF b NONVIOLENCE b	American Friends Service Committee. SPEAK TRUTH TO POWER: A QUAKER SEARCH FOR AN ALTERNATIVE TO VIOLENCE. Philadelphia: American Friends Service Committee, 1955.
EDUCATION b,c	American Friends Service Committee. WORKBOOK TO END WAR. Philadelphia: American Friends Service Committee, 1973.
	American Friends Service Committee, see Lauter, Paul; Yarrow, Mike.
DEVELOPMENT 1,c	Amin, Samir. ACCUMULATION ON A WORLD SCALE: A CRITIQUE OF THE THEORY OF UNDERDEVELOPMENT. New York: Monthly Review Press, 1974 (Orig. pub. in French, 1971).

I. ORGANIZATION 2,a I. POLITICAL 2 MEDIATION a	Andemicael, Berhanykun. PEACEFUL SETTLEMENT AMONG AFRICAN STATES: ROLES OF THE UNITED NATIONS AND THE ORGANIZATION OF AFRICAN UNITY. New York: United Nations Institute for Training and Research, 1972.
	Anders, Gunther, see Eatherly, Claude.
DEVELOPMENT 6 I. ECONOMIC 1	Anderson, Jan Otto. STUDIES IN THE THEORY OF UNEQUAL EXCHANGE BETWEEN NATIONS. Abo, Finland: Abo Akademi, 1976.
	Anderson, Nels, see Reigrotski, Erich.
MILITARY 5	Andpreski, Stanislav. MILITARY ORGANIZATION AND SOCIETY. Berkeley: University of California Press, 1968.
MILITARY 5,6	Angell, Norman. THE GREAT ILLUSION: A STUDY OF THE RELATION OF MILITARY POWER IN NATIONS TO THEIR ECONOMIC AND SOCIAL ADVANTAGE. New York: Garland, 1971 (Orig. pub., 1911).
FUTURES 1,b	Angell, Robert C. "National Support for World Order." JOURNAL OF CONFLICT RESOLUTION, 17, 3 (September 1973), 429-454.
TRANSNATIONAL 5, 6,b	Angell, Robert C. PEACE ON THE MARCH: TRANSNATIONAL PARTICIPATION. New York: Van Nostrand Reinhold, 1969.
CONFLICT 1,5	Angell, Robert C. "The Sociology of Human Conflict," in E. McNeil, Editor, THE NATURE OF HUMAN CONFLICT. Englewood Cliffs, N.J.: Prentice-Hall, 1965.

VIOLENCE b	Ardrey, Robert. THE TERRITORIAL IMPERATIVE. New York: Atheneum, 1966.
LIBERATION 1,2,4 WARFARE 1,c	Arendt, Hannah. ON REVOLUTION. New York: Viking, 1963.
CONFLICT 1 RESEARCH a VIOLENCE 1,7	Arendt, Hannah. ON VIOLENCE. New York: Harcourt, Brace and World, 1970.
CONFLICT 1 MEDIATION 1	Argyris, Chris. INTERVENTION THEORY AND METHOD. Reading, Mass.: Addison-Wesley, 1970.
I. POLITICAL 2 WARFARE a	Aron, Raymond. THE CENTURY OF TOTAL WAR. Boston: Beacon, 1955.
I. POLITICAL 1,2 WARFARE 1,2	Aron, Raymond. ON WAR: ATOMIC WEAPONS AND GLOBAL DIPLOMACY. Garden City, N.Y.: Doubleday, 1958.
I. POLITICAL 1,2	Aron, Raymond. PEACE AND WAR: A THEORY OF INTERNATIONAL RELATIONS. Translated from the French by Richard Howard and Annette Baker Fox. Garden City, N.Y.: Doubleday, 1966.
DEVELOPMENT b PROTEST 2 RESOURCES 3,a	Artin, Tom. EARTH TALK: INDEPENDENT VOICES ON THE ENVIRONMENT. New York: Grossman, 1973.
	Aspin, Les, <u>see</u> Kemp, Jack.
CONFLICT 3,f I. POLITICAL 3 WARFARE 3	Azar, Edward E., and Thomas J. Sloan. DIMENSIONS OF INTERACTION: A SOURCE BOOK FOR THE STUDY OF THE BEHAVIOR OF 31 NATIONS FROM 1948 THROUGH 1973. Pittsburgh: International Studies Association, 1975.
CONFLICT 3 WARFARE 1,b,c	Azar, Edward E. PROBE FOR PEACE: SMALL-STATE HOSTILITIES. Minneapolis: Burgess, 1973.

INTERNATIONAL 1	Azar, Edward E., Editor. THE REVIEW OF PEACE SCIENCE. Volume 1. Oakville, Ontario: Canadian Peace Research Institute, 1973.
CONFLICT f	Azar, Edward E., and Joseph Ben-Dak, Editors. THEORY AND PRACTICE OF EVENTS ANALYSIS. New York: Gordon and Breach, 1975.
WARFARE 2,c	Baechler, Jean. REVOLUTION. Translated by Jean Vickers. New York: Harper and Row, 1976.
	Bahry, Donna, <u>see</u> Kanet, Roger E.
EDUCATION 1 RESEARCH b	Baines, James. "The Peace Paradigm." WHOLE EARTH PAPERS, 1, 1 (1977).
ATTITUDES b,2 NONVIOLENCE b	Bainton, Roland H. CHRISTIAN ATTITUDES TOWARD WAR AND PEACE. New York: Abingdon, 1960.
DEVELOPMENT 2	Bairoch, Paul. THE ECONOMIC DEVELOPMENT OF THE THIRD WORLD SINCE 1900. Translated from the fourth French edition by Cynthia Postan. Berkeley: University of California Press, 1975.
DEVELOPMENT b I. ECONOMIC 2	Baklanoff, Eric N. EXPROPRIATION OF U.S. INVESTMENTS IN CUBA, MEXICO, AND CHILE. New York: Praeger, 1975.
I. POLITICAL d	Ball, Nicole. REGIONAL CONFLICTS AND THE INTERNATIONAL SYSTEM. Sussex, England: Institute for the Study of International Organization, University of Sussex, 1974.

PROTEST 2	Bannan, John F., and Rosemary S. Bannan. LAW, MORALITY AND VIETNAM: THE PEACE MILITANTS AND THE COURTS. Bloomington: Indiana University Press, 1974.
	Bannan, Rosemary S., <u>see</u> Bannan, John F.
DEVELOPMENT 2	Barbera, Henry. RICH NATIONS AND POOR IN PEACE AND WAR: CONTINUITY AND CHANGE IN THE DEVELOPMENT HIERARCHY OF SEVENTY NATIONS FROM 1913 THROUGH 1952. Lexington, Mass.: Lexington Books, 1973.
CONFLICT 1,5,7 CRISIS a	Bard, Morton. "Family Intervention Police Teams as a Community Mental Health Resource." JOURNAL OF CRIMINAL LAW, CRIMINOLOGY AND POLICE SCIENCE, 60 (1969), 247-250.
CONFLICT 5,7 MEDIATION 1	Bard, Morton, and Joseph Zacher. "The Prevention of Family Violence: Dilemmas of Community Intervention." JOURNAL OF MARRIAGE AND THE FAMILY, 33, 4 (November 1971), 677-682.
I. POLITICAL a	Barghoorn, Frederick C. DETENTE AND THE DEMOCRATIC MOVEMENT IN THE USSR. Riverside, N.J.: Free Press, 1976.
INTEGRATION 2 I. LAW 1,2,b	Barkun, Michael. LAW WITHOUT SANCTIONS: ORDER IN PRIMITIVE SOCIETIES AND THE WORLD COMMUNITY. New Haven, Conn.: Yale University Press, 1968.
ARMS 2,4 RESOURCES b	Barnaby, Frank. THE NUCLEAR AGE. Cambridge, Mass.: MIT Press, 1975.
	Barnes, M., <u>see</u> Komorita, S.

ARMS 6 DISARMAMENT 7 MILITARY 1,2	Barnet, Richard J. THE ECONOMY OF DEATH. New York: Atheneum, 1969.
TRANSNATIONAL 6	Barnet, Richard J., and Ronald E. Müller. GLOBAL REACH: THE POWER OF THE MULTINATIONAL CORPORATIONS. New York: Simon and Schuster, Touchstone Books, 1974.
CONFLICT 2,4 DEVELOPMENT b I. POLITICAL 1,2 LIBERATION 2,4	Barnet, Richard J. INTERVENTION AND REVOLUTION: AMERICA'S CONFRONTATION WITH INSURGENT MOVEMENTS AROUND THE WORLD. New York: Meridian, 1968.
DISARMAMENT b INTERNATIONAL 1, 4,a WARFARE 1,a	Barnet, Richard J. ROOTS OF WAR, THE MEN AND INSTITUTIONS BEHIND U.S. FOREIGN POLICY. New York: Atheneum, 1972.
I. POLITICAL 1,a WARFARE 1,a	Barnett, Frank R., William C. Mott, and John C. Nef, Editors. PEACE AND WAR IN THE MODERN AGE: PREMISES, MYTHS AND REALITIES. Garden City, N.Y.: Anchor, 1965.
WARFARE 1,2,3	Barringer, Richard E., and Robert K. Ramers. WAR: PATTERNS OF CONFLICT. Foreword by Quincy Wright. Cambridge, Mass.: MIT Press, 1972.
I. POLITICAL 1 RESEARCH a	Barsegov, Yuri, and Rustem Khairov. "A Study of the Problems of Peace." JOURNAL OF PEACE RESEARCH, 10, 1 and 2 (1973), 71-80.
MEDIATION 2,b	Barston, Ronald. "Problems in International Peacekeeping: The Case of Cyprus." INTERNATIONAL RELATIONS (London), 3, 11 (May 1971), 928-940.
	Barth, William, <u>see</u> Kelman, Herbert C.

DISARMAMENT a	Barton, John H., and Lawrence D. Weiler, Editors. INTERNATIONAL ARMS CONTROL: ISSUES AND AGREEMENTS. Stanford, Calif.: Stanford University Press, 1976.
CONFLICT 1,2,3,g MEDIATION 1,2,3	Bartos, Otomar J. "How Predictable Are Negotiations?" JOURNAL OF CONFLICT RESOLUTION, 11, 4 (December 1967), 481-496.
CONFLICT 1,b	Bartos, Otomar J. PROCESS AND OUTCOMES OF NEGOTIATIONS. New York: Columbia University Press, 1974.
I. POLITICAL 1	Baudissin, Wolf. "Changes in the Meaning of Military and Political Concepts of Peace." SOCIAL RESEARCH, 42, 1 (Spring 1975), 112-125.
TERRORISM 1,c	Bauman, Carol E. THE DIPLOMATIC KIDNAPPINGS. The Hague: Martinus Nijoff, 1973.
FUTURES 2 PROTEST 2 TRANSNATIONAL 2, a,b	Beales, A. C. F. THE HISTORY OF PEACE: A SHORT ACCOUNT OF THE ORGANIZED MOVEMENTS FOR INTERNATIONAL PEACE. London: Dial Press, 1931.
NONVIOLENCE 1,2 PROTEST 1,2	Beckwith, George C., Editor. THE BOOK OF PEACE: A COLLECTION OF ESSAYS ON WAR AND PEACE. Englewood, N.J.: Jerome S. Ozer, 1972 (Orig. pub., 1845).
WARFARE 2,3	Beer, Francis A. HOW MUCH WAR IN HISTORY: DEFINITIONS, ESTIMATES, EXTRAPOLATIONS AND TRENDS. Beverly Hills, Calif.: Sage, 1974.

FUTURES b NONVIOLENCE 4 PROTEST 1	Beitz, Charles R., and A. Michael Washburn. CREATING THE FUTURE: A GUIDE TO LIVING AND WORKING FOR SOCIAL CHANGE. New York: Bantam Books, 1974.
ARMS 4,5,6 CIVILIAN DEF 1 FUTURES b I. LAW 1,a I. ORGANIZATION 1,2 I. POLITICAL 1 NONVIOLENCE 1,2 PROTEST 1,2 VIOLENCE 7,b WARFARE 1	Beitz, Charles R., and Theodore Herman, Editors. PEACE AND WAR. San Francisco: Freeman, 1973.
CRISIS 1,2,4 MEDIATION 2,a	Bell, Coral. THE CONVENTIONS OF CRISIS: A STUDY IN DIPLOMATIC MANAGEMENT. Oxford, England: Oxford University Press, for the Royal Institute of International Affairs, 1971.
LIBERATION 1,a	Bell, J. Bowyer. ON REVOLT: STRATEGIES OF NATIONAL LIBERATION. Cambridge, Mass.: Harvard University Press, 1976.
TERRORISM c	Bell, J. Bowyer. TRANSNATIONAL TERROR. Washington, D.C. and Stanford, Calif.: American Enterprise Institute for Public Policy Research and Hoover Institute on War, Revolution and Peace, 1975.
VIOLENCE 4,5	Ben-Dak, Joseph D., Editor. THE FUTURE OF COLLECTIVE VIOLENCE: SOCIETAL AND INTERNATIONAL PERSPECTIVES. Lund, Sweden: Studentliteratur, 1974.
	Ben-Dak, Joseph D., <u>see</u> Azar, Edward E.

DEVELOPMENT 2,4, 5,6	Bendix, Reinhard. NATION-BUILDING AND CITIZENSHIP: STUDIES OF OUR CHANGING SOCIAL ORDER. New York: Doubleday, 1969.
ATTITUDES b	Benedict, Marion J. THE GOD OF THE OLD TESTAMENT IN RELATION TO WAR. New York: Bureau of Publications, Teachers College, Columbia University, 1927.
	Benjamin, R. W., see Bobrow, Davis B.
	Bennis, Warren, see Schein, Edgar.
DISARMAMENT 2,b	Benoit, Emile. "Cutting Back Military Spending: The Vietnam Withdrawal and the Recession." ANNALS OF THE AMERICAN ACADEMY OF POLITICAL AND SOCIAL SCIENCES, 406 (March 1973), 73-79.
ARMS 6 DEVELOPMENT 2,3,b	Benoit, Emile. DEFENSE AND ECONOMIC GROWTH IN DEVELOPING COUNTRIES. Lexington, Mass.: Lexington Books, 1973.
DISARMAMENT 1,6	Benoit, Emile, and Kenneth E. Boulding, Editors. DISARMAMENT AND THE ECONOMY. New York: Harper and Row, 1963.
DISARMAMENT 1,6,a INTEGRATION 6 I. ECONOMIC 5	Benoit, Emile, and Nils Petter Gleditsch, Editors. DISARMAMENT AND WORLD ECONOMIC INTERDEPENDENCE. New York: Columbia University Press, 1967.
DISARMAMENT 6	Benoit, Emile. "Ending the Arms Race as an Economic Problem." REVIOTA INTERNAZIONALE DI SCIENZE ECONOMICHE E COMMERCIALI, 15, 6 (1968), 533-549.

	Bentsi-Enchill, Kwamena, see Smock, David R.
CONFLICT 1,3 EDUCATION b,c FUTURES 1,a I. POLITICAL 1,d WARFARE 1,3	Beres, Louis René, and Harry R. Targ. CONSTRUCTING ALTERNATIVE WORLD FUTURES: REORDERING THE PLANET. Cambridge, Mass.: Schenkman, 1978.
FUTURES 1,b	Beres, Louis René, and Harry R. Targ, Editors. PLANNING ALTERNATIVE WORLD FUTURES: VALUES, METHODS, AND MODELS. New York: Praeger, 1975.
I. ECONOMIC 4 I. POLITICAL 6	Bergsten, C. Fred, and Lawrence B. Krause, Editors. WORLD POLITICS AND INTERNATIONAL ECONOMICS. Washington, D.C.: Brookings Institution, 1975.
DISARMAMENT 6	Berkowitz, Marvin. THE CONVERSION OF MILITARY-ORIENTED RESEARCH AND DEVELOPMENT TO CIVILIAN USES. New York: Praeger, 1970.
LIBERATION 4,c MILITARY 4	Berman, Paul. REVOLUTIONARY ORGANIZATION: INSTITUTION-BUILDING WITHIN THE PEOPLE'S LIBERATION ARMED FORCES. Lexington, Mass.: Lexington Books, 1974.
CONFLICT 1,5	Bernard, Jessie. "Parties and Issues in Conflict." JOURNAL OF CONFLICT RESOLUTION, 1, 2 (June 1957), 111-121.
WARFARE 1,2	Bernard, L. L. WAR AND ITS CAUSES. New York: Henry Holt, 1944.
INTEGRATION 4 I. LAW 2 I. POLITICAL d	Bernier, Ivan. INTERNATIONAL LEGAL ASPECTS OF FEDERALISM. London: Longman Group, 1973.
DEVELOPMENT c FUTURES b I. ECONOMICS 1 RESOURCES b	Bhagwati, Jagdish N., Editor. ECONOMICS AND WORLD ORDER FROM THE 1970's TO THE 1990's. New York: Macmillan, 1972.

DEVELOPMENT 4,6 I. ECONOMIC 4	Bhattacharya, Anindya K. FOREIGN TRADE AND INTERNATIONAL DEVELOPMENT. Lexington, Mass.: Lexington Books, 1976.
MEDIATION b NONVIOLENCE 1,2,a	Bhave, Vinoba. SHANTI SENA. Translated by Marjorie Sykes. Kashi, India: Akhil Bharat Sarva Seva Sangh Drakashan, 1961.
	Biderman, Albert D., see Myer, Samuel.
DEVELOPMENT 3,4 MILITARY 1,2,5,c	Bienen, Henry, Editor. THE MILITARY AND MODERNIZATION. Chicago: Aldine/Atherton, 1971.
CONFLICT 2,5,a,d I. ORGANIZATION 2	Bissell, Richard E. APARTHEID AND INTERNATIONAL ORGANIZATIONS. Boulder, Colo.: Westview, 1977.
	Bitterman, Albert D., see Crawford, Elisabeth T.
	Blackey, Robert, See Paynton, Clifford T.
RESOURCES 4,6,b	Blair, John Malcolm. THE CONTROL OF OIL. New York: Pantheon, 1976.
I. ECONOMIC 4	Blake, David H., and Robert S. Walters. THE POLITICS OF GLOBAL ECONOMIC RELATIONS. Englewood Cliffs, N.J.: Prentice-Hall, 1976.
	Blalock, Ann, see Northwood, L. K.
ATTITUDES 5 CONFLICT 1,4,5,6,7 INTEGRATION 1,4,5,6,7 MEDIATION 1	Blau, Peter M. EXCHANGE AND POWER IN SOCIAL LIFE. New York: Wiley, 1964.

CONFLICT 1,5,7 MEDIATION 1	Blood, Robert. "Resolving Family Conflicts." JOURNAL OF CONFLICT RESOLUTION, 5, 2 (June 1960), 209-219.
I. ORGANIZATION 1 MEDIATION b MILITARY b	Bloomfield, Lincoln P. THE POWER TO KEEP PEACE, TODAY AND IN A WORLD WITHOUT WAR. Berkeley, Calif.: World Without War Council, 1971 (Orig. pub., 1964).
	Bloomstein, Charles, <u>see</u> Nesbitt, William.
	Blumberg, Herbert H., <u>see</u> Hare, A. Paul (1970, 1977).
CONFLICT 2 INTEGRATION b I. LAW 2 RESEARCH a	Boasson, Charles, Editor, in association with Max Nurock. THE CHANGING INTERNATIONAL COMMUNITY: SOME PROBLEMS OF ITS LAWS, STRUCTURES, PEACE RESEARCH AND THE MIDDLE EAST CONFLICT. Essays in honour of Marion Mushkat. The Hague: Mouton, 1973.
CONFLICT 4 DEVELOPMENT a WARFARE 1	Bobrow, Davis B., P. T. Hopmann, R. W. Benjamin, and D. A. Sylvan. "The Impact of Foreign Assistance on National Development and International Conflict." JOURNAL OF PEACE SCIENCE 1, 1 (Autumn 1973), 39-60.
INTEGRATION 5 I. LAW 5 I. ORGANIZATION 5 I. POLITICAL 5	Bogardus, Emory. "The Sociology of a Structured Peace." SOCIOLOGY AND SOCIAL RESEARCH, 44, 5 (May-June 1960), 352-356.
I. LAW b WARFARE 1,2	Bohannan, Paul, Editor. LAW AND WARFARE: STUDIES IN THE ANTHROPOLOGY OF CONFLICT. New York: Natural History Press, 1967.

DISARMAMENT 1,3 VIOLENCE a	Bolte, Charles. THE PRICE OF PEACE. Boston: Beacon, 1956.
DISARMAMENT 6	Bolton, Roger E., Editor. DEFENSE AND DISARMAMENT: THE ECONOMICS OF TRANSITION. Englewood Cliffs, N.J.: Prentice-Hall, 1966.
CONFLICT a I. LAW 1,2 WARFARE 1	Bond, James Edward. THE RULES OF RIOT: INTERNAL CONFLICT AND THE LAW OF WAR. Princeton, N.J.: Princeton University Press, 1974.
CONFLICT 1,2 NONVIOLENCE 1,2,b VIOLENCE 1	Bondurant, Joan V., Editor. CONFLICT: VIOLENCE AND NONVIOLENCE. New York: Atherton, 1971.
NONVIOLENCE 1,2,b	Bondurant, Joan V. CONQUEST OF VIOLENCE: THE GANDHIAN PHILOSOPHY OF CONFLICT. Berkeley: University of California Press, 1965.
CONFLICT 1,2,5,7 I. POLITICAL 1,7,a MEDIATION 2,a NONVIOLENCE 1	Bonoma, Thomas V., and Thomas W. Milburn, Issue Editors. "Social Conflict." JOURNAL OF SOCIAL ISSUES, 33, 1 (Winter 1977).
EDUCATION 2 RESEARCH a,b	Bornstein, Rita. "Interdisciplinary Approach to War-Peace Studies." ENGLISH JOURNAL, 63, 2 (February 1974), 64-66.
CIVILIAN DEF 1,2,b NONVIOLENCE 4	Boserup, Anders, and Andrew Mack. WAR WITHOUT WEAPONS: NONVIOLENCE IN NATIONAL DEFENSE. New York: Schocken Books, 1975.
CONFLICT 1,5	Bottomore, Thomas. "Sociological Theory and the Study of Social Conflict," in J. C. McKinney and Edward A. Tiryakian, Editors, THEORETICAL SOCIOLOGY. New York: Appleton-Century Crofts, 1970.

NONVIOLENCE 7,c	Boulding, Elise. "The Child and Nonviolent Social Change," in Christoph Wulf, Editor, HANDBOOK ON PEACE EDUCATION. Frankfurt: Education Committee of the International Peace Research Association. Also in Israel Charny, Editor, STRATEGIES AGAINST NONVIOLENT CHANGE, 1978.
ATTITUDES 1,2,b INTEGRATION 1 I. POLITICAL 2	Boulding, Elise, Issue Editor. "Conflict and Community in the International System." JOURNAL OF SOCIAL ISSUES, 27, 1 (January 1967).
MEDIATION 1	Boulding, Elise. "Further Reflections on Conflict Management," in Robert Kahn and Elise Boulding, Editors, POWER AND CONFLICT IN ORGANIZATIONS. New York: Basic Books, 1964.
TRANSNATIONAL 1, 3,5	Boulding, Elise. "The Measurement of Cultural Potentials for Transnationalism." JOURNAL OF PEACE RESEARCH, 11, 3 (1975), 189-202.
RESEARCH a,b	Boulding, Elise. "Peace Research: Dialectics and Development." JOURNAL OF CONFLICT RESOLUTION, 16, 4 (December 1972), 469-475.
RESEARCH a	Boulding, Elise. "Peace Research in Asia." OUR GENERATION AGAINST NUCLEAR WAR, 3, 2 (1964), 62-65..
RESEARCH a	Boulding, Elise, and Raimo Väyrynen. "Peace Research: The Infant Discipline," in Stein Rokkan, Editor, A QUARTER CENTURY OF SOCIAL SCIENCE. Paris: United Nations Educational, Scientific, and Cultural Organization.

INTEGRATION 1,2 RESEARCH a,b	Boulding, Elise. "The Study of Conflict and Community in the International System: Summary and Challenges to Research." JOURNAL OF SOCIAL ISSUES, 23, 1 (January 1967), 144-158.
	Boulding, Elise, see Fink, Clinton F.; Kahn, Robert L.
CONFLICT 1 I. POLITICAL 1,6, a,b	Boulding, Kenneth E. COLLECTED PAPERS. Volume 5: INTERNATIONAL SYSTEMS: PEACE, CONFLICT RESOLUTION AND POLITICS. Edited by Larry D. Singell. Boulder: Colorado Associated University Press, 1975.
CONFLICT 1,5,6 I. POLITICAL 6,a	Boulding, Kenneth E. CONFLICT AND DEFENSE: A GENERAL THEORY. New York: Harper, 1962.
DEVELOPMENT 1,2, b,c I. ECONOMIC 4	Boulding, Kenneth E., and Tapan Mukerjee, Editors. ECONOMIC IMPERIALISM: A BOOK OF READINGS. Ann Arbor: University of Michigan Press, 1972.
DISARMAMENT 6 I. ECONOMIC 4 RESOURCES 6	Boulding, Kenneth E. THE ECONOMICS OF PEACE. New York: Prentice-Hall, 1945. Reprinted: Freeport, N.Y.: Books for Libraries Press, 1972.
CONFLICT 1 EDUCATION d I. POLITICAL 1	Boulding, Kenneth E. "The Learning of Peace." INTERNATIONAL STUDIES NOTES, 1, 2 (Summer 1974), 1-8.
DISARMAMENT 6 MILITARY 1,6	Boulding, Kenneth E., Editor. PEACE AND THE WAR INDUSTRY. Second Edition. New Brunswick, N.J.: E. P. Dutton, for Transaction Books, 1973 (First edition, 1970).
RESEARCH a	Boulding, Kenneth E. "Peace Research." INTERNATIONAL SOCIAL SCIENCE JOURNAL, 29, 4 (1977), 601-614.

CONFLICT 1	Boulding, Kenneth E. "The Power of Nonconflict." JOURNAL OF SOCIAL ISSUES, 33, 1 (Winter 1977), 22-33.
CONFLICT 1,4 I. ORGANIZATION 1 I. POLITICAL 1,a,c MEDIATION 1 NONVIOLENCE 1,4 RESEARCH b	Boulding, Kenneth E. STABLE PEACE. Austin: University of Texas Press, 1978.
	Boulding, Kenneth E., see Benoit, Emile.
WARFARE 1	Bouthoul, Gaston, and Rene Carrère. LE DEFI DE LA GUERRE, 1740-1974. Paris: Presses Universitaires de France, 1976.
WARFARE 1	Bouthoul, Gaston. LE PHENOMENE-GUERRE. Paris: Petite Bibliotheque Payot, 1962.
	Bowlby, John, see Durbin, E. F. M.
ATTITUDES 1,2,4 CONFLICT 1,2,4 I. LAW 1,b I. ORGANIZATION 1, 2,a I. POLITICAL 1,2	Bozeman, Adda B. CONFLICT IN AFRICA: CONCEPTS AND REALITIES. Princeton, N.J.: Princeton University Press, 1976.
	Brady, Richard A., see Geutzkow, Harold S.
ATTITUDES 2 MILITARY 1,4,5 VIOLENCE 1,5,7,8 WARFARE 1,2	Bramson, Leon, and George W. Goethals, Editors. WAR: STUDIES FROM PSYCHOLOGY, SOCIOLOGY, ANTHROPOLOGY. New York: Basic Books, 1968 (First edition, 1964).
	Brehmer, Berndt, see Hammond, Kenneth.
	Brent, Harry, see Lutz, William.

CONFLICT 1,5,6 LIBERATION 1 MEDIATION 1 VIOLENCE 7	Brickman, Philip, Editor. SOCIAL CONFLICT: READINGS IN RULE STRUCTURES AND CONFLICT RELATIONSHIPS. Lexington, Mass.: D. C. Heath, 1974.
NONVIOLENCE 2,b	Brock, Peter. PACIFISM IN EUROPE TO 1914. Princeton, N.J.: Princeton University Press, 1972.
NONVIOLENCE 2,b	Brock, Peter. PACIFISM IN THE UNITED STATES: FROM THE COLONIAL ERA TO THE FIRST WORLD WAR. Princeton, N.J.: Princeton University Press, 1968.
NONVIOLENCE 2,b	Brock, Peter. TWENTIETH CENTURY PACIFISM. New York: Van Nostrand Reinhold, 1970.
ATTITUDES 1,2,a	Bronfenbrenner, Urie. "The Mirror Image in Soviet-American Relations: A Social Psychologists's Report." JOURNAL OF SOCIAL ISSUES, 17, 3 (1961), 45-50.
	Brown, Bert R., see Rubin, Jeffrey Z.
RESOURCES 6,d SECURITY e	Brown, Lester R. REDEFINING NATIONAL SECURITY. Washington, D.C.: Worldwatch Institute, 1978.
CRISIS 6 FUTURES 1 RESOURCES 1,2,6, a-d	Brown, Lester R. THE TWENTY-NINTH DAY: ACCOMMODATING HUMAN NEEDS AND NUMBERS TO THE EARTH'S RESOURCES. New York: W. W. Norton, 1978.
RESOURCES a	Brown, Lester R. WORLD WITHOUT BORDERS. New York: Random House, 1972.

VIOLENCE 2	Brown, Richard Maxwell. STRAIN OF VIOLENCE: HISTORICAL STUDIES OF AMERICAN VIOLENCE AND VIGILANTISM. New York: Oxford University Press, 1975.
	Bruck, H. W., <u>see</u> Snyder, Richard C.
NONVIOLENCE 1,2	Bruyn, Severyn T., and Paula Raymon, Editors. CREATIVE CONFLICT IN SOCIETY: NON-VIOLENT THEORY AND ACTION. New York: Wiley, 1978.
ATTITUDES 1,2,4	Buber, Martin. ISRAEL AND THE WORLD: ESSAYS IN A TIME OF CRISIS. New York: Schocken Books, 1963 (Orig. pub., 1945).
CONFLICT 1 VIOLENCE 1,5 WARFARE 1,2	Buchan, Alastair. WAR IN MODERN SOCIETY. New York: Harper and Row, 1968.
ATTITUDES 4 I. POLITICAL 7	Buchanan, William, and Hadley Cantril. HOW NATIONS SEE EACH OTHER. Urbana: University of Illinois Press, 1953.
	Buehrig, Edward H., <u>see</u> Lepawsky, Albert.
SECURITY a,b,e TRANSNATIONAL 5	Buergenthal, Thomas, and Judith V. Torney. INTERNATIONAL HUMAN RIGHTS AND INTERNATIONAL EDUCATION. Washington, D.C.: U.S. National Commission for UNESCO, Department of State, 1976.
ARMS a	Bull, Hedley. THE CONTROL OF THE ARMS RACE. New York: Praeger, 1965.
	Bullough, Vern L., <u>see</u> Naroll, Raoul.

MEDIATION 2,b MILITARY b	Burns, Arthur L., and Nina Heathcote. PEACE KEEPING BY UNITED NATIONS FORCES, FROM SUEZ TO THE CONGO. New York: Praeger, for Center of International Studies, Princeton University, 1963.
	Burrell, Sidney, see Deutsch, Karl.
CONFLICT 1,2,3	Burton, John W. CONFLICT AND COMMUNICATION. New York: Macmillan, 1969.
I. ORGANIZATION 1 I. POLITICAL 1,b RESEARCH b	Burton, John W. INTERNATIONAL RELATIONS: A GENERAL THEORY. London: Cambridge University Press, 1965.
DISARMAMENT 1,a I. POLITICAL a	Burton, John W. PEACE THEORY: PRECONDITIONS OF DISARMAMENT. New York: Alfred Knopf, 1962.
CONFLICT 1 MEDIATION 1	Burton, John W. "Resolution of Conflict." INTERNATIONAL STUDIES QUARTERLY, 16, 1 (March 1972), 5-30.
INTEGRATION 1 I. POLITICAL 1	Burton, John W. WORLD SOCIETY. London: Cambridge University Press, 1972.
CONFLICT 2,3,4,a I. POLITICAL 2,3 MEDIATION 2,3	Butterworth, Robert Lyle, with Margaret E. Scranton. MANAGING INTERSTATE CONFLICT, 1945-74: DATA WITH SYNOPSES. Pittsburgh: University Center for International Studies, University of Pittsburgh, 1976.
WARFARE 1	Byley, B., et.al. MARXISM-LENINISM ON WAR AND ARMY. Moscow: Progress Publishers, 1972.

NONVIOLENCE b	Cadoux, Cecil John. CHRISTIAN PACIFISM RE-EXAMINED. New York: Garland, 1971 (Orig. pub., 1940).
FUTURES 3 WARFARE a,c	Calder, Nigel, Editor. UNLESS PEACE COMES: A SCIENTIFIC FORECAST OF NEW WEAPONS. New York: Viking, 1968.
I. ORGANIZATION 1 RESOURCES 1,a,b,c TRANSNATIONAL 1	Caldwell, Lynton K. IN DEFENSE OF EARTH: INTERNATIONAL PROTECTION OF THE BIOSPHERE. Bloomington: Indiana University Press, 1972.
FUTURES 1 VIOLENCE 1	Camus, Albert. NEITHER VICTIMS NOR EXECUTIONERS. Berkeley, Calif.: World Without War Council, 1960. Also in Peter Mayer, Editor, THE PACIFIST CONSCIENCE.
CONFLICT 3 CRISIS 2 WARFARE 2,3	Canadian Peace Research Institute. "Predictions of War: Three Studies from the Canadian Peace Research and Education Association Conference of June, 1973; Kingston, Ontario." PEACE RESEARCH REVIEWS, 5, 4 (February 1974).
ATTITUDES 1,2,a	Cantril, Hadley. THE PATTERN OF HUMAN CONCERNS. New Brunswick, N.J.: Rutgers University Press, 1965.
ARMS 1 I. POLITICAL 1 WARFARE 1	Cantril, Hadley, Editor. TENSIONS THAT CAUSE WARS. Urbana: University of Illinois Press, 1950.
	Cantril, Hadley, see Buchanan, William.
CONFLICT 1,3,e	Caplow, Theodore. TWO AGAINST ONE: COALITIONS IN TRIADS. Englewood Cliffs, N.J.: Prentice-Hall, 1968.

ARMS 1,2 CONFLICT 1 DISARMAMENT 1,a WARFARE a	Carlton, David, and Carlo Schaerf, Editors. THE DYNAMICS OF THE ARMS RACE. London: Croom Helm, 1975.
EDUCATION a,b,c FUTURES 1,2 MEDIATION 1,2 NONVIOLENCE 1,2, 7,c RESEARCH b	Carpenter, Susan, Editor. REPERTOIRE OF PEACEMAKING-SKILLS. Boulder, Colo.: Susan Carpenter, 1977. Distributed by Consortium on Peace Research, Education and Development.
	Carrere, Rene, see Bouthoul, Gaston.
CRISIS c WARFARE 1,2	Carroll, Berenice A. "How Wars End: An Analysis of Some Current Hypothesis." JOURNAL OF PEACE RESEARCH, 6, 4 (1969), 295-322.
NONVIOLENCE 5,7	Case, Clarence March. NON-VIOLENT COERCION: A STUDY IN METHODS OF SOCIAL PRESSURE. Introduction by A. Paul Hare. New York: Garland, 1971 (Orig. pub., 1923).
INTEGRATION 5 TRANSNATIONAL 5	Casmir, Fred L., Editor. INTER-CULTURAL AND INTERNATIONAL COMMUNICATION. Washington, D.C.: University Press of America, 1978.
EDUCATION a,b,c	Center for War/Peace Studies, New York. "Teaching About War, Peace, Conflict, and Change." INTERCOM, 13, 2 (March/April 1971), 24-63.
CONFLICT 2 MEDIATION 2,a	Chalmers, William E., and Gerald W. Cormick, Editors. RACIAL CONFLICT AND NEGOTIATIONS: PERSPECTIVES AND FIRST CASE STUDIES. Ann Arbor: Institute of Labor and Industrial Relations, University of Michigan and Wayne State University, 1971.

Chammah, Albert M., *see* Rapoport, Anatol.

NONVIOLENCE b,c

Charny, Israel W. "The Psychotherapist as Teacher of an Ethic of Non-Violence." VOICES, THE ART AND SCIENCE OF PSYCHOTHERAPY, 3, 4 (1967), 57-66.

EDUCATION 1
FUTURES 1
INTEGRATION 1
NONVIOLENCE 5,7,c
VIOLENCE 2,7

Charny, Israel W., Editor. STRATEGIES AGAINST VIOLENCE: DESIGN FOR NONVIOLENT CHANGE. Boulder, Colo.: Westview, 1978.

NONVIOLENCE 2,4,5
PROTEST 2
WARFARE 2

Chatfield, Charles. FOR PEACE AND JUSTICE: PACIFISM IN AMERICA, 1914-1941. Boston: Beacon, 1973.

NONVIOLENCE 2,5,7
PROTEST 2

Chatfield, Charles, Issue Editor. "Peace Movements in America." AMERICAN STUDIES, 13, 1 (Spring 1972).

CONFLICT b
NONVIOLENCE 1

Chatterjee, Bishwa B. "Search for an Appropriate Game Model for Gandhian Satyagraha." JOURNAL OF PEACE RESEARCH, 11, 1 (1974), 21-29.

DEVELOPMENT c
FUTURES 1
RESEARCH a

Chaudhr, Mohammed A. "Peace Research and the Developing Countries." JOURNAL OF PEACE RESEARCH, 5, 4 (1968), 365-374.

DEVELOPMENT 1,2,3,4,6,b,d

Chenery, Hollis, *et.al*. REDISTRIBUTION WITH GROWTH: POLICIES TO IMPROVE INCOME DISTRIBUTION IN DEVELOPING COUNTRIES IN THE CONTEXT OF ECONOMIC GROWTH. New York: Oxford University Press, for the World Bank and the Institute of Development Studies, University of Sussex, 1974.

I. POLITICAL a	Choucri, Nazli, and Robert C. North. NATIONS IN CONFLICT: NATIONAL GROWTH AND INTERNATIONAL VIOLENCE. San Francisco: W. H. Freeman, 1975.
RESOURCES 4,a,b	Choucri, Nazli. "Population, Resources and Technology: Political Implications of the Environmental Crisis." INTERNATIONAL ORGANIZATION, 26, 2 (Spring 1972), 175-212.
I. LAW a,d	Clark, Grenville, and Louis B. Sohn. INTRODUCTION TO WORLD PEACE THROUGH WORLD LAW. Revised Edition. Chicago: World Without War Publications, 1973. This volume also includes essays by: Saul Mendlovitz and Thomas Weiss, Elizabeth Mann Borgese, and Robert Pickus and Robert Woito.
I. LAW a,d I. ORGANIZATION 1	Clark, Grenville, and Louis B. Sohn. WORLD PEACE THROUGH WORLD LAW: TWO ALTERNATIVE PLANS. Third Edition revised and enlarged. Cambridge, Mass.: Harvard University Press, 1966 (First edition, 1960).
FUTURES 2 WARFARE 1	Clarke, Ignatius Frederick. VOICES PROPHESYING WAR: 1763-1984. London: Oxford University Press, 1966.
CONFLICT 1 RESOURCES a VIOLENCE 7 WARFARE a	Clarke, Robin. THE SCIENCE OF WAR AND PEACE. New York: McGraw-Hill, 1972.
ARMS 4,5,6 WARFARE 1,2	Clarkson, Jesse D., and Thomas Cochran. WAR AS A SOCIAL INSTITUTION. New York: Columbia University Press, 1941.

DISARMAMENT 1,a,b
I. ORGANIZATION 1,a

Claude, Inis L., Jr. SWORDS INTO PLOWSHARES: THE PROBLEMS AND PROGRESS OF INTERNATIONAL ORGANIZATION. Third Edition, revised. New York: Random House, 1964 (First edition, 1956).

SECURITY a,b

Claude, Richard P., Editor. COMPARATIVE HUMAN RIGHTS. Baltimore: Johns Hopkins Press, 1976.

CONFLICT 1,7
WARFARE 1,2

Clausewitz, Carl von. ON WAR. Edited and translated by Michael Howard and Peter Paret. Introductory Essays by Peter Paret, Michael Howard, and Bernard Brodie; with a Commentary by Bernard Brodie. Prepared under the auspices of the Center of International Studies, Princeton University. Princeton, N.J.: Princeton University Press, 1977.

CONFLICT 1
WARFARE 1,2

Clausewitz, Carl von. WAR, POLITICS, AND POWER. Edited and translated with an Introduction by E. M. Collins. Chicago: Henry Regnery, 1962.

INTEGRATION 1,2,3
I. ORGANIZATION 1,2,3

Cobb, Roger W., and Charles Elder. INTERNATIONAL COMMUNITY: A REGIONAL AND GLOBAL STUDY. New York: Holt, Rinehart and Winston, 1970.

ARMS 2
WARFARE 1,2

Coblentz, Stanton A. FROM ARROW TO ATOM BOMB. New York: Beechhurst, 1953.

CRISIS 2,b
WARFARE 2

Coblentz, Stanton A. TEN CRISES IN CIVILIZATION. Chicago: Follett, 1965.

Cochran, Thomas, see Clarkson, Jesse D.

MEDIATION 1,a	Coddington, Allan. THEORIES OF THE BARGAINING PROCESS. Chicago: Aldine, 1968.
DEVELOPMENT b,c I. ECONOMIC 4	Cohen, Benjamin J. THE QUESTION OF IMPERIALISM: THE POLITICAL ECONOMY OF DOMINANCE AND DEPENDENCE. New York: Basic Books, 1973.
I. POLITICAL 2,a	Cohen, Bernard C. THE INFLUENCE OF NON-GOVERNMENTAL GROUPS ON FOREIGN POLICY MAKING. Princeton, N.J.: Center of International Studies, Princeton University, for the World Peace Foundation, 1959.
CONFLICT 2 MEDIATION a	Cohen, Stephen P., Herbert C. Kelman, Frederick D. Miller, and Bruce L. Smith. "Evolving Intergroup Techniques for Conflict Resolution: An Israeli-Palestinian Pilot Workshop." JOURNAL OF SOCIAL ISSUES, 33, 1 (1977), 165-189.
CONFLICT 1,2	Coleman, James S. COMMUNITY CONFLICT. New York: Free Press, 1957.
RESEARCH c	Coleman, James S. POLICY RESEARCH IN THE SOCIAL SCIENCES. Morristown, N.Y.: General Learning Press, 1972.
RESEARCH a	Converse, Elizabeth. "The War of All Against All: A Review of the Journal of Conflict Resolution." JOURNAL OF CONFLICT RESOLUTION, 12, 4 (December 1968), 471-532.
MILITARY 1	Cook, Fred. THE WARFARE STATE. New York: Macmillan, 1962.

NONVIOLENCE 1,a,c
PROTEST 2,4

Cooper, William, A. Paul Hare, Theodore Olson, and Charles Walker. NONVIOLENCE AND SOCIAL CHANGE: FOUR ESSAYS. Haverford, Pa.: Haverford College.

EDUCATION 1
NONVIOLENCE a,b,c
PROTEST b

Coover, Virginia, Ellen Deacon, Charles Esser, and Christopher Moore. RESOURCE MANUAL FOR A LIVING REVOLUTION. Philadelphia: Movement for a New Society, 1978.

I. ECONOMIC 1,2
RESOURCES b
TRANSNATIONAL 6

Corbet, Hugh, and Robert Jackson, Editors. IN SEARCH OF A NEW WORLD ECONOMIC ORDER. New York: Wiley/Halsted, 1974.

Cormick, Gerald W., see Chalmers, William E.

DEVELOPMENT 4
MILITARY 2,c
VIOLENCE 2,4

Cortese, Charles F. MODERNIZATION, THREAT, AND THE POWER OF THE MILITARY. Beverly Hills, Calif.: Sage, 1976.

ATTITUDES 1,2
CONFLICT 1,2

Coser, Lewis, Issue Editor. "Collective Violence and Civil Conflict." JOURNAL OF SOCIAL ISSUES, 28, 1 (1972).

CONFLICT 1
INTEGRATION 1,2

Coser, Lewis. CONTINUITIES IN THE STUDY OF SOCIAL CONFLICT. Glencoe, Ill.: Free Press, 1967.

CONFLICT 1
INTEGRATION 1
RESEARCH a

Coser, Lewis. THE FUNCTION OF SOCIAL CONFLICT. Glencoe, Ill.: Free Press, 1956.

MEDIATION a

Coser, Lewis. "Peaceful Settlements and the Dysfunctions of Secrecy." JOURNAL OF CONFLICT RESOLUTION, 7, 3 (September 1963), 246-253.

CONFLICT 1 CRISIS c	Coser, Lewis. "The Termination of Conflict." JOURNAL OF CONFLICT RESOLUTION, 5, 4 (December 1961), 347-353.
FUTURES 1 WARFARE a	Cousins, Norman. IN PLACE OF FOLLY. New York: Harper, 1961.
CONFLICT 1 DISARMAMENT 1,a,b I. POLITICAL a,f	Cox, Arthur Macy. THE DYNAMICS OF DÉTENTE: HOW TO END THE ARMS RACE. New York: W. W. Norton, 1976.
CONFLICT 1,2	Crain, Robert, Elihu Katz, and Donald Rosenthal. THE POLITICS OF COMMUNITY CONFLICT: THE FLUORIDATION DECISION. New York: Bobbs-Merrill, 1969.
RESEARCH c,d	Crawford, Elisabeth T., and Albert D. Bitterman, Editors. SOCIAL SCIENTISTS AND INTERNATIONAL AFFAIRS: A CASE FOR A SOCIOLOGY OF SOCIAL SCIENCE. New York: Wiley, 1969.
CONFLICT 2,5,d PROTEST 1,2 VIOLENCE 5	Critchley, T. A. THE CONQUEST OF VIOLENCE: ORDER AND LIBERTY IN BRITAIN. New York: Shocken Books, 1970.
CONFLICT 1,2,4,5,6 DEVELOPMENT 2,4,b,c,d MEDIATION 1,2	Curle, Adam. MAKING PEACE. London: Tavistock, 1971.
ATTITUDES 1,2	Curle, Adam. MYSTICS AND MILITANTS. New York: Harper, 1973.
	Curtis, H. W., see Knight, Douglas.
ATTITUDE 3,5	Cutler, Neal E. "Generational Succession as a Source of Foreign Policy Attitudes." JOURNAL OF PEACE RESEARCH, 7 (1970), 33-48.

Czmanski, Stanislaw, see Isard, Walter.

Dahl, Barbara B., see McCubbin, Hamilton I.

FUTURES 1 — Dahl, Norman C., and Jerome B. Weisner, Editors. WORLD CHANGE AND WORLD SECURITY. Cambridge, Mass.: MIT Press, 1978.

CONFLICT 1,5,d — Dahrendorf, Ralf. CLASS AND CLASS CONFLICT IN INDUSTRIAL SOCIETY. Stanford, Calif.: Stanford University Press, 1959.

CONFLICT 1,4,5,d — Dahrendorf, Ralf. CONFLICT AFTER CLASS: NEW PERSPECTIVES ON THE THEORY OF SOCIAL AND POLITICAL CONFLICT. London: Longmans, 1967.

CONFLICT 1,5 — Dahrendorf, Ralf. "Toward a Theory of Social Conflict." JOURNAL OF CONFLICT RESOLUTION, 2, 2 (June 1958), 170-183.

CONFLICT 1,2,c; DEVELOPMENT 1,2,b; RESEARCH a; VIOLENCE 1,2 — Dasgupta, Sugata. PROBLEMS OF PEACE RESEARCH: A THIRD WORLD VIEW. New Delhi: Indian Council of Peace Research, 1974.

CONFLICT 2,5; NONVIOLENCE 1,6 — Dasgupta, Sugata. SOCIAL WORK AND SOCIAL CHANGE. Boston: Porter Sargeant, 1968.

WARFARE 1,2 — Davie, Maurice R. THE EVOLUTION OF WAR: A STUDY OF ITS ROLE IN EARLY SOCIETIES. New Haven, Conn.: Yale University Press, 1929.

VIOLENCE 7
WARFARE 2,c

Davies, James Chowning. "The J-Curve of Rising and Declining Satisfactions as a Cause of Some Great Revolutions and a Contained Rebellion," in Hugh Davis Graham and Ted Robert Gurr, Editors, VIOLENCE IN AMERICA: HISTORICAL AND COMPARATIVE PERSPECTIVES. New York: Bantam Books, 1969.

VIOLENCE 1,7
WARFARE 1,2,c

Davies, James Chowning, Editor. WHEN MEN REVOLT--AND WHY: A READER IN POLITICAL VIOLENCE AND REVOLUTION. New York: Free Press, 1971.

CONFLICT 1,7
INTEGRATION 7

Davison, W. Phillips. MASS COMMUNICATION AND CONFLICT RESOLUTION: THE ROLE OF THE INFORMATION MEDIA IN THE ADVANCEMENT OF INTERNATIONAL UNDERSTANDING. New York: Praeger, 1974.

CONFLICT 1,7

Dawkins, Richard. THE SELFISH GENE. New York: Oxford University Press, 1976.

Deacon, Ellen, see Coover, Virginia.

DEVELOPMENT 6,c
WARFARE 1,2

Debray, Regis. REVOLUTION IN THE REVOLUTION? ARMED STRUGGLE AND POLITICAL STRUGGLE IN LATIN AMERICA. Translated by Bobbye Ortiz. New York: Grove, 1967.

RESEARCH a,b

Dedring, Juergen. RECENT ADVANCES IN PEACE AND CONFLICT RESEARCH: A CRITICAL SURVEY. Foreword by Elise Boulding; Preface by J. David Singer. Beverly Hills, Calif.: Sage, 1976.

LIBERATION 2,a,c
NONVIOLENCE 2,a,b
PROTEST 2

Dellinger, Dave. REVOLUTIONARY NONVIOLENCE: ESSAYS BY DAVE DELLINGER. Indianapolis: Bobbs-Merrill, 1970.

CONFLICT 1,2,5,7	DeReuck, Anthony. CONFLICT IN SOCIETY. Boston: Little, Brown, 1966.
DEVELOPMENT 1,2,c FUTURES 1 I. POLITICAL 2	De Riencourt, Amaury. THE AMERICAN EMPIRE. New York: Dial, 1968.
CONFLICT 5 DEVELOPMENT 1,d NONVIOLENCE a	Desai, Narayan. TOWARDS A NON-VIOLENT REVOLUTION. Rajghat Varanasi, India: Sarva Seva Sangh Prakashan, 1972.
RESEARCH a,b WARFARE 1	Deutsch, Karl W., and Dieter Senghaas. "A Framework for a Theory of War and Peace," in Albert Lepawsky, *et.al.*, Editors, THE SEARCH FOR WORLD ORDER. New York: Appleton-Century-Crofts, 1971.
INTEGRATION 2,a I. ORGANIZATION 1,2	Deutsch, Karl W., and Sidney Burrell. POLITICAL COMMUNITY AND THE NORTH ATLANTIC AREA: INTERNATIONAL ORGANIZATION IN THE LIGHT OF HISTORICAL EXPERIENCE. Princeton, N.J.: Princeton University Press, 1967.
INTEGRATION 4 I. POLITICAL 5	Deutsch, Karl W. POLITICAL COMMUNITY AT THE INTERNATIONAL LEVEL: PROBLEMS OF DEFINITION AND MEASUREMENT. Garden City, N.Y.: Doubleday, 1954.
	Deutsch, Karl W., *see* Russett, Bruce M.
CONFLICT 1 MEDIATION a	Deutsch, Morton. THE RESOLUTION OF CONFLICT: CONSTRUCTIVE AND DESTRUCTIVE PROCESSES. New Haven, Conn.: Yale University Press, 1973.
	Deutsch, Morton, *see* Muney, Barbara; Wright, Quincy.

EDUCATION b,c	Diablo Valley Education Project. SELECTED WAR/PEACE CURRICULUM UNITS AVAILABLE FOR HIGH SCHOOL LEVEL TEACHING. Orinda, Calif.: Diablo Valley Education Project, 1971.
	Dickie, Paul M., *see* Lauter, Geza P.
CONFLICT 5	Dodson, Dan E. "The Creative Role of Conflict in Intergroup Relations." MERRILL-PALMER QUARTERLY (Summer 1958), 188-195.
CONFLICT 6 DEVELOPMENT 5,6, 7,d	Dolci, Danilo. REPORT FROM PALERMO. Translated by P. D. Cummings; introduction by Aldous Huxley. New York: Viking, 1970.
VIOLENCE 1,2,3,7,b	Dollard, John, Leonard Dobb, N. E. Miller, A. H. Mowrer, and R. R. Sears. FRUSTRATION AND AGGRESSION. New Haven, Conn.: Yale University Press, 1939.
	Dolman, Anthony J., *see* Tinbergen, Jan.
ARMS 2 I. POLITICAL a MILITARY 1,2,c	Donovan, J. S. MILITARISM USA. New York: Scribner's, 1970.
CONFLICT 1,2 INTEGRATION 7,a	Doob, Leonard, *et al*. RESOLVING CONFLICT IN AFRICA: THE FERMEDA WORKSHOP. New Haven, Conn.: Yale University Press, 1970.
	Doob, Leonard, *see* Dollard, John.
ARMS 2,4,6 MILITARY 6	Dörfer, Ingemar. SYSTEM 37 VIGGEN: ARMS, TECHNOLOGY AND THE DOMESTICATION OF GLORY. Oslo: Universitetsforlaget, 1973.

I. LAW a	Douglas, William O. INTERNATIONAL DISSENT: SIX STEPS TO WORLD PEACE. New York: Random House, 1971.
RESOURCES a,c	Dreachslin, Janice, Sylvia Messer, Marion Edman, and Lillian Genser. "Living on Spaceship Earth." SCHOLASTIC TEACHER (Elementary Teachers Edition) (April-May 1974), 25-31.
MEDIATION a	Druckman, Daniel. HUMAN FACTORS IN INTERNATIONAL NEGOTIATIONS. New York: Academy for Educational Development, 1971.
DISARMAMENT 6 MILITARY 1,2,c SECURITY a	Dumas, Lloyd J. "Thirty Years of the Arms Race: The Deterioration of Economic Strength and Military Security." PEACE AND CHANGE, 4, 2 (1977), 3-9.
LIBERATION 2 WARFARE 1,c	Dunn, John M. MODERN REVOLUTIONS: AN INTRODUCTION TO THE ANALYSIS OF A POLITICAL PHENOMENON. New York: Cambridge University Press, 1972.
VIOLENCE 1,2,7,a,b	Durbin, E. F. M., and John Bowlby. "Personal Aggressiveness and War," in WAR AND DEMOCRACY. London: Kegan Paul, Teuch, Trubner, 1938.
INTEGRATION 1 I. POLITICAL 1	Durkheim, Emile, et.al. SUR L'INTERNATIONALISME. New York: Garland, 1971 (Orig. pub., 1906).
	Duston, R., see Johnson D.
WARFARE 2	Eatherly, Claude, and Gunther Anders. BURNING CONSCIENCE: THE CASE OF THE HIROSHIMA PILOT CLAUDE EATHERLY TOLD IN HIS LETTERS TO GUNTHER ANDERS. New York: Monthly Review Press, 1962.

ATTITUDES 3,a NONVIOLENCE 1,2,b RESEARCH a	Eckhardt, William. COMPASSION: TOWARD A SCIENCE OF VALUE. Oakville, Ontario: Canadian Peace Research Institute, 1972.
ATTITUDES 1,2,3, 4,5	Eckhardt, William, and Theo. F. Lentz. "Factors of War Peace Attitudes." PEACE RESEARCH REVIEWS, 1, 5 (October 1967).
CONFLICT a DEVELOPMENT c I. ECONOMIC 1,2, 4,5 LIBERATION 2 VIOLENCE 2	Eckhardt, William, and Christopher Young. GOVERNMENTS UNDER FIRE: CIVIL CONFLICT AND IMPERIALISM. New Haven, Conn.: Human Relations Area Files Press, 1977.
ATTITUDES 1,2,4 I. POLITICAL a	Eckhardt, William, and Ralph K. White. "A Test of the Mirror Mirror-Image Hypothesis: Kennedy and Krushchev." JOURNAL OF CONFLICT RESOLUTION, 11, 3 (September 1967), 325-332.
	Eckhardt, William, see Newcombe, Alan G.
DISARMAMENT 6 RESEARCH a	Edelstein, Michael. THE ECONOMIC IMPACT OF MILITARY SPENDING. New York: Council on Economic Priorities, 1977.
	Edman, Marion, see Dreachslin, Janice.
MEDIATION 3,a	Edmead, Frank. ANALYSIS AND PREDICTION IN INTERNATIONAL MEDIATION. New York: United Nations Institute for Training and Research, 1971.
DISARMAMENT 4,a FUTURES 1 I. POLITICAL 1	Edwards, David V. ARMS CONTROL IN INTERNATIONAL POLITICS. New York: Holt, Rinehart and Winston, 1969.

CONFLICT 1,4 FUTURES 1,b	Edwards, David V. CREATING A NEW WORLD POLITICS: FROM CONFLICT TO COOPERATION. New York: David McKay, 1973.
WARFARE c	Edwards, Lyford P. THE NATURAL HISTORY OF REVOLUTION. Chicago: University of Chicago Press, 1927.
I. ECONOMIC 4 I. POLITICAL 6 TRANSNATIONAL 6	Eells, Richard. GLOBAL CORPORATIONS: THE EMERGING SYSTEM OF WORLD ECONOMIC POWER. Revised Edition with an Epilogue. New York: Free Press, 1976.
	Effrat, Andrew, see Hare, A. Paul.
	Egge, Bjørn, see Rikhye, Indar Jit.
	Ehrlich, Paul R., see Pirages, Dennis C.
I. LAW d	Eide, Asbjørn. "International Law, Dominance, and the Use of Force." JOURNAL OF PEACE RESEARCH 11, 1 (1974), 1-20.
CONFLICT h I. LAW 2 SECURITY a	Eide, Asbjørn, and August Schou, Editors. INTERNATIONAL PROTECTION OF HUMAN RIGHTS. New York: Wiley, 1968.
RESEARCH b,d	Eide, Asbjørn. "A Value-based Approach: Methods and Problems in Peace Research." INTERNATIONAL SOCIAL SCIENCE JOURNAL, 26, 1 (1974), 119-133.
TRANSNATIONAL 5	Eilde, Ingrid, Editor. STUDENTS AS LINKS BETWEEN CULTURES: A CROSS-CULTURAL STUDY BASED ON UNESCO STUDIES. Oslo: Universitetsforlaget, 1970.

DISARMAMENT a FUTURES b NONVIOLENCE b	Einstein, Albert. EINSTEIN ON PEACE. Edited by Otto Nathau, and Heinz Norden, with preface by Bertrand Russell. New York: Simon and Schuster, 1960.
	Elder, Charles, see Cobb, Roger W.
DEVELOPMENT b I. ECONOMIC 2	Elliot, Charles. DO THE POOR SUBSIDIZE THE RICH? Geneva: World Council of Churches, 1973.
CONFLICT 2	Elliot, R. S. P., and John Hickie. ULSTER, A CASE STUDY IN CONFLICT THEORY. New York: St. Martin's, 1972.
DISARMAMENT 6	Elliott, Dave, Mary Kaldor, Dan Smith, and Ron Smith. ALTERNATIVE WORK FOR MILITARY INDUSTRIES. London: Richardson Institute for Conflict and Peace Research, 1977.
WARFARE 1,2	Engels, Friedrich. ENGELS AS MILITARY CRITIC: ARTICLES BY FRIEDRICH ENGELS. Edited by W. H. Choloner and W. D. Henderson. New York: Barnes and Noble, 1959.
ATTITUDES 2,b I. LAW 2,d	Eppstein, John. THE CATHOLIC TRADITION OF THE LAW OF NATIONS. London: Burns, Oates, and Washbourne, 1935.
ARMS 2,b DISARMAMENT 2,a FUTURES 1	Epstein, William. THE LAST CHANCE: NUCLEAR PROLIFERATION AND ARMS CONTROL. New York: Free Press, 1976.

DEVELOPMENT 2,6 INTEGRATION 4 I. LAW 2,c I. ECONOMIC a I. POLITICAL 1,2	Erb, Guy F., and Valeriana Kallab, Editors. BEYOND DEPENDENCY: THE DEVELOPING WORLD SPEAKS OUT. New York: Praeger, in cooperation with the Overseas Development Council, 1975.
NONVIOLENCE 2,7,a, b,c PROTEST 2	Erikson, Erik. GANDHI'S TRUTH: ON THE ORIGINS OF MILITANT NONVIOLENCE. New York: W. W. Norton, 1969.
INTEGRATION 2,7	Espinas, Alfred Victor. DES SOCIETIES ANIMALS. Fourth Edition. Bibliotheque des Philosophie Contemporain. Paris: G. Bailliere, 1925 (Orig. pub., 1877).
	Esser, Charles, see Coover, Virginia.
ARMS a CONFLICT 1,4,7 CRISIS 7,a,c DISARMAMENT 4,5 MEDIATION a	Etzioni, Amitai. THE HARD WAY TO PEACE: A NEW STRATEGY. New York: Collier Books, 1962.
RESEARCH b	Etzioni, Amitai. "Non-Conventional Uses of Sociology as Illustrated by Peace Research," in Paul F. Lazarsfeld, et al., Editors, THE USES OF SOCIOLOGY. New York: Basic Books, 1967.
CONFLICT 1	Etzioni, Amitai. "On Self-Encapsulating Conflicts." JOURNAL OF CONFLICT RESOLUTION, 8, 3 (September 1964), 242-255.
INTEGRATION 1,4	Etzioni, Amitai. POLITICAL UNIFICATION. New York: Holt, Rinehart and Winston, 1965.

ATTITUDES 2 CONFLICT 1 DISARMAMENT 4,6 MEDIATION a WARFARE 1,a	Etzioni, Amitai, and Martin Wenglinsky, Editors. WAR AND ITS PREVENTION. New York: Harper and Row, 1970.
CONFLICT 2,3,b,g MEDIATION 1,2	Evan, William M., and John A. MacDougall. "Interorganizational Conflict: A Labor-Management Bargaining Experiment." JOURNAL OF CONFLICT RESOLUTION, 11, 4 (December 1967), 398-413.
	Evan, William M., see Wright, Quincy.
	Ezkiel, Raphael S., see Kelman, Herbert C.
MEDIATION b MILITARY a	Fabian, Larry L. SOLDIERS WITHOUT ENEMIES. Washington, D.C.: Brookings Institution, 1971.
DISARMAMENT a FUTURES 1 I. LAW a,d	Falk, Richard A. LEGAL ORDER IN A VIOLENT WORLD. Princeton, N.J.: Princeton University Press, 1968.
DISARMAMENT 4,5,6,b I. POLITICAL a	Falk, Richard A. NUCLEAR POLICY AND WORLD ORDER: WHY DENUCLEARIZATION. New York: Institute for World Order, 1978.
FUTURES b INTEGRATION 4 I. LAW a I. POLITICAL d	Falk, Richard A., and Saul H. Mendlovitz, Editors. REGIONAL POLITICS AND WORLD ORDER. San Francisco: W. H. Freeman, 1973.
FUTURES 1,b	Falk, Richard A. A STUDY OF FUTURE WORLDS. Amsterdam: North-Holland, 1975.
FUTURES b RESOURCES a	Falk, Richard A. THIS ENDANGERED PLANET: PROSPECTS AND PROPOSALS FOR HUMAN SURVIVAL. New York: Random House, 1971.

CRISIS 4,7
I. POLITICAL 7,a

Falkowski, Lawrence. PRESIDENTS, SECRETARIES OF STATE, AND CRISIS MANAGEMENT IN U.S. FOREIGN RELATIONS: A MODEL AND PREDICTIVE ANALYSIS. Boulder, Colo.: Westview, 1978.

VIOLENCE 1,2,4
WARFARE c

Fall, Bernard. THE TWO VIETNAMS: A POLITICAL AND MILITARY ANALYSIS. New York: Praeger, 1966.

DEVELOPMENT c

Fanon, Frantz. DYING COLONIALISM. New York: Grove, 1965.

CONFLICT 1
LIBERATION 1,4,6

Fanon, Frantz. THE WRETCHED OF THE EARTH. New York: Grove, 1963.

ATTITUDES 1,4
I. POLITICAL 1

Farrell, John C., Issue Editor. "Image and Reality in World Politics." JOURNAL OF INTERNATIONAL AFFAIRS, 21, 1 (1967).

CONFLICT 1,4,5
VIOLENCE 1,4,5,6,7,b
WARFARE 1,c

Feierabend, Ivo K., Rosalind L. Feierabend, and Ted Robert Gurr, Editors. ANGER, VIOLENCE AND POLITICS: THEORIES AND RESEARCH. New York: Prentice-Hall, 1972.

Feierabend, Rosalind L., see Feierabend, Ivo K.

Feivenson, Harold A., see Greenwood, Ted.

ARMS 2

Feld, Bernard T., et al. IMPACT OF NEW TECHNOLOGIES ON THE ARMS RACE. Cambridge, Mass.: MIT Press, 1971.

MILITARY 2
VIOLENCE 1

Feld, Maury D. THE STRUCTURE OF VIOLENCE. Beverly Hills, Calif.: Sage, 1977.

I. ORGANIZATION 1,2

Feng Yang Chai. CONSULTATION AND CONSENSUS IN THE SECURITY COUNCIL. New York: United Nations Institute for Training and Research, 1971.

EDUCATION a,b,c	Feraru, Anne T. INTERNATIONAL CONFLICT. St. Louis: Consortium for International Studies Education, 1974.
VIOLENCE 1,a	Feshbach, Seymour, and Robert D. Singer. TELEVISION AND AGGRESSION. San Francisco: Jossey-Bass, 1971.
I. ECONOMIC 1,2, 4,a I. ORGANIZATION 1,2 TRANSNATIONAL 6	Finger, Seymour Maxwell, and Joseph R. Harbert. U.S. POLICY IN INTERNATIONAL INSTITUTIONS: DEFINING REASONABLE OPTIONS IN AN UNREASONABLE WORLD. Boulder, Colo.: Westview, 1978.
RESEARCH a	Fink, Clinton F., and Elise Boulding, Issue Editors. "Peace Research in Transition: A Symposium." JOURNAL OF CONFLICT RESOLUTION, 16, 4 (December 1972).
CONFLICT 1,5	Fink, Clinton F. "Some Conceptual Difficulties in the Theory of Social Conflict." JOURNAL OF CONFLICT RESOLUTION, 12, 4 (December 1968), 412-460.
I. ORGANIZATION 3 TRANSNATIONAL 5	Fischer, Heintz-Dietrich, and John C. Merrill. INTERNATIONAL COMMUNICATION MEDIA, CHANNELS, FUNCTIONS. New York: Hastings House, 1970.
ATTITUDES a CONFLICT 2	Fisher, Roger. DEAR ISRAELIS, DEAR ARABS: A WORKING APPROACH TO PEACE. New York: Harper and Row, 1972.
CONFLICT 1 I. POLITICAL 1	Fisher, Roger, Editor. INTERNATIONAL CONFLICT AND BEHAVIORAL SCIENCE: THE CRAIGVILLE PAPERS. New York: Basic Books, 1964.

CONFLICT 1 I. POLITICAL 1	Fisher, Roger. INTERNATIONAL CONFLICT FOR BEGINNERS. New York: Harper and Row, 1969.
MEDIATION 1	Fisher, Ronald J. "Third Party Consultation: A Method for the Study and Resolution of Conflict." JOURNAL OF CONFLICT RESOLUTION, 16, 1 (March 1972), 67-94.
CONFLICT 2 I. POLITICAL 1,2	Fitzgerald, Frances. FIRE IN THE LAKE: THE VIETNAMESE AND THE AMERICANS IN VIETNAM. Boston: Little, Brown, 1972.
	Fogel, Lawrence J., see Knight, Douglas.
MEDIATION 1,2	Ford Foundation. NEW APPROACHES TO CONFLICT RESOLUTION: A FORD FOUNDATION REPORT. New York: Ford Foundation, May 1978.
VIOLENCE 7	Fornari, Franco. THE PSYCHOANALYSIS OF WAR. Bloomington: Indiana University Press, 1975.
DEVELOPMENT 4	Fossum, Egil. "Political Development and Strategies for Change." JOURNAL OF PEACE RESEARCH, 7, 1 (1970), 17-32.
	Fox, Robin, see Tiger, Lionel.
VIOLENCE 5,6,7 WARFARE 1,2	Fox, William T. R., Issue Editor. "How Wars End." ANNALS OF THE AMERICAN ACADEMY OF POLITICAL AND SOCIAL SCIENCE, 392 (November 1970).
I. POLITICAL 2,f	Franck, Thomas M., and Edward Weisband. WORLD POLITICS: VERBAL STRATEGY AMONG THE SUPERPOWERS. New York: Oxford University Press, 1971.

DEVELOPMENT 1,4,6, b,c I. ECONOMIC 5,a	Frank, André. ON CAPITALIST UNDERDEVELOPMENT. New York: Oxford University Press, 1976.
CONFLICT 7 DISARMAMENT 7 VIOLENCE 7 WARFARE 1	Frank, Jerome D. SANITY AND SURVIVAL: PSYCHOLOGICAL ASPECTS OF WAR AND PEACE. New York: Vintage, 1967.
	Frenkel-Brunswick, Else, see Adorno, Theodore W.
CONFLICT 1,7,a	Freud, Sigmund. CIVILIZATION AND ITS DISCONTENTS. Translated by James Strachey. New York: Norton, 1961 (Orig. pub., 1930).
CONFLICT 1,7,a WARFARE 1	Freud, Sigmund. CIVILISATION, WAR AND DEATH. Edited by John Rickman. London: Hogarth, 1968.
CONFLICT 1 VIOLENCE 1 WARFARE 1	Fried, Morton, Marvin Harris, and Robert Murphy, Editors. WAR: THE ANTHROPLOGY OF ARMED CONFLICT AND AGGRESSION. Garden City, N.Y.: Natural History Press, 1968.
	Friends Peace Committee, Philadelphia, see Walker, Charles; Shivers, Lynn, and T. Olson.
VIOLENCE 1,7,a	Fromm, Erich. THE ANATOMY OF HUMAN DESTRUCTIVENESS. New York: Holt, Rinehart and Winston, 1973.
CONFLICT 1,7 MEDIATION 1	Frost, Joyce. INTERPERSONAL CONFLICT. Dubuque, Iowa: Brown, 1978.
MEDIATION b MILITARY b	Frydenberg, Per, Editor. PEACE-KEEPING, EXPERIENCE AND EVALUATION. Oslo: Norwegian Institute of International Affairs, 1964.

MILITARY 4,5,6	Fulbright, J. William. THE PENTAGON PROPAGANDA MACHINE. New York: Liveright, 1970.
WARFARE 1,2	Fuller, J. F. C. THE CONDUCT OF WAR: 1789-1961. New Brunswick, N.J.: Rutgers University Press, 1961.
INTEGRATION 4,5,6	Galtung, Johan, Editor. CO-OPERATION IN EUROPE. Oslo: Universitetsforlaget, 1970.
I. ORGANIZATION 2,a	Galtung, Johan. THE EUROPEAN COMMUNITY: A SUPERPOWER IN THE MAKING. London: Allen and Unwin, 1973.
DEVELOPMENT 1,c	Galtung, Johan. "A Structural Theory of Imperialism." JOURNAL OF PEACE RESEARCH, 8, 2 (1971), 81-117.
FUTURES 1,b I. ORGANIZATION 1 TRANSNATIONAL 1	Galtung, Johan. THE TRUE WORLDS. New York: Free Press, 1978.
RESEARCH a VIOLENCE 1	Galtung, Johan. "Violence, Peace and Peace Research." JOURNAL OF PEACE RESEARCH, 6, 3 (1969), 67-92.
	Galtung, Johan, <u>see</u> Jungk, Robert.
PROTEST 1,2,5,a,b VIOLENCE 2	Gamson, William A. THE STRATEGY OF SOCIAL PROTEST. Homewood, Ill.: Dorsey, 1975.
CONFLICT 1,e	Gamson, William A. "A Theory of Coalition Formation." AMERICAN SOCIOLOGICAL REVIEW, 26, 3 (June 1961), 373-382.
ATTITUDES a CRISIS 1,2	Gamson, William A., and Andre Modigliani. UNTANGLING THE COLD WAR: A STRATEGY FOR TESTING RIVAL THEORIES. Boston: Little, Brown, 1971.

NONVIOLENCE 1,a,b	Gandhi, Mohandas K. ALL MEN ARE BROTHERS: LIFE AND THOUGHTS OF MAHATMA GANDHI. Edited by K. Kripalani. Mystic, Conn.: Lawrence Verry, 1969.
NONVIOLENCE 2	Gandhi, Mohandas K. AN AUTOBIOGRAPHY: THE STORY OF MY EXPERIEMENTS WITH TRUTH. Boston: Beacon, 1957.
NONVIOLENCE 1,2	Gandhi, Mohandas K. NONVIOLENCE IN PEACE AND WAR. New York: Garland, 1971 (Orig. pub. in India, 1942).
NONVIOLENCE 1 PROTEST 1	Gandhi, Mohandas K. NONVIOLENT RESISTANCE (Satyagraha). New York: Schocken Books, 1963.
	Gandhi, Mohandas K. For works about Gandhi, <u>see</u> Bhave, Vinoba; Bondurant, Joan V.; Chatterjee, Bishwa B.; Erikson, Erik; Ganguli, Birendra Nath; Gregg, Richard B. (1971, 1929); Naess, Arne; Sharp, Gene; Shridharani, Krishnalal; Tinker, Jerry.
RESEARCH 1	Gandhian Institute of Studies. Special Issue: "Peace Research." INTERDISCIPLINE, 10, 4 (Winter 1973).
NONVIOLENCE 1,2	Ganguli, Birendra Nath. GANDHI'S SOCIAL PHILOSOPHY: PERSPECTIVE AND RELEVANCE. New York: Wiley, 1973.
WARFARE 2,b	Gann, Lewis. GUERRILLAS IN HISTORY. Stanford, Calif.: Hoover Institution Press, 1971.
ARMS 5	Gardiner, Robert W. THE COOL ARM OF DESTRUCTION: MODERN WEAPONS AND MORAL INSENSIBILITY. Philadelphia: Westminster, 1974.

EDUCATION b,c TERRORISM 4	Garrigan, Timothy B., and George A. Lopez. TERRORISM: A PROBLEM OF POLITICAL VIOLENCE. Columbus: Ohio State University Press, 1978.
ATTITUDES b EDUCATION b SECURITY a,b	Genser, Lillian, Editor. THE CHILD'S DECLARATION OF RIGHTS AND RESPONSIBILITIES AND THE DECLARATION OF THE RIGHTS OF THE CHILD. Detroit: Wayne State University Press, 1978.
	Genser, Lillian, see Dreachslin, Janice.
CONFLICT 2 I. POLITICAL 1,2	George, Alexander L., David K. Hall, and William E. Simons. THE LIMITS OF COERCIVE DIPLOMACY: LAOS-CUBA-VIETNAM. Boston: Little, Brown, 1971.
LIBERATION c WARFARE 1,c	Giap, Vo Nguyen. THE MILITARY ART OF PEOPLE'S WAR: SELECTED WRITINGS OF GENERAL VO NGUYEN GIAP. Edited by Russell Stetler. New York: Monthly Review Press, 1970.
CONFLICT 3 DEVELOPMENT 3	Gillespie J., and Betty Nesvold, Editors. MACROQUANTITATIVE ANALYSIS: CONFLICT, DEVELOPMENT, AND DEMOCRATIZATION. Beverly Hills, Calif.: Sage, 1971.
I. ECONOMIC 4 I. POLITICAL 6 TRANSNATIONAL 6	Gilpin, Robert. U.S. POWER AND THE MULTINATIONAL CORPORATION: THE POLITICAL THEORY OF FOREIGN DIRECT INVESTMENT. New York: Basic Books, 1975.
VIOLENCE 1,5 WARFARE 1	Ginsberg, Robert, Editor. THE CRITIQUE OF WAR. Chicago: Henry Regnery, 1969.
VIOLENCE 1,7,b WARFARE 1	Givens, R. Dale, and Martin A. Nettleship, Editors. DISCUSSIONS ON WAR AND HUMAN AGGRESSION. The Hague: Mouton, 1976.

	Givens, R. Dale, <u>see</u> Nettleship, Martin A.
	Gleditsch, Nils Petter, <u>see</u> Benoit, Emile.
MILITARY 1,5,c	Glick, Edward. SOLDIERS, SCHOLARS AND SOCIETY: THE SOCIAL IMPACT OF THE AMERICAN MILITARY. Pacific Palisades, Calif.: Goodyear, 1971.
	Godoy, Horacio H., <u>see</u> Lagos, Gustavo.
	Goethals, George W., <u>see</u> Bramson, Leon.
MILITARY 7	Goldman, Nancy, and David R. Segal, Editors. THE SOCIAL PSYCHOLOGY OF MILITARY SERVICE. Beverly Hills, Calif.: Sage, 1976.
ARMS 1 INTEGRATION 1,4 I. POLITICAL 1	Goldman, Ralph M. "A Transactional Theory of Political Integration and Arms Control." AMERICAN POLITICAL SCIENCE REVIEW, 63, 3 (September 1969), 719-733.
CONFLICT 1	Goode, William J. "The Place of Force in Human Society." AMERICAN SOCIOLOGICAL REVIEW, 37, 5 (October 1972), 507-519.
I. ORGANIZATION 1,2 I. POLITICAL 1	Goodrich, Leland M., and David A. Kay, Editors. THE POLITICS OF INTERNATIONAL ORGANIZATION. Madison: University of Wisconsin Press, 1973.
ARMS RACE 2 DISARMAMENT 4 I. LAW a	Gotlieb, Allan. DISARMAMENT AND INTERNATIONAL LAW. Lindsay, Ontario, Canada: John Deyell, International, 1965.

DEVELOPMENT 2,d LIBERATION 1	Goulet, Denis. A NEW MORAL ORDER: STUDIES IN DEVELOPMENT ETHICS AND LIBERATION THEOLOGY. Foreword by Paulo Freire. Maryknoll, N.Y.: Orbis, 1974.
ARMS b	Gray, Colin S. "New Weapons and the Resort to Force." INTERNATIONAL JOURNAL, 30, 2 (Spring 1975), 238-258.
ARMS a CONFLICT 1,h I. POLITICAL f	Gray, Colin S. THE SOVIET-AMERICAN ARMS RACE. Lexington, Mass.: Lexington Books, 1976.
MILITARY 1 VIOLENCE 7 WARFARE 1	Gray, J. Glen. THE WARRIORS: REFLECTIONS ON MEN IN BATTLE. New York: Harper and Row, 1967.
TRANSNATIONAL 6	Gray, Richard B., Editor. INTERNATIONAL SECURITY SYSTEMS: CONCEPTS OF MODELS OF WORLD ORDER. Itasca, Ill.: F. E. Peacock, 1969.
ARMS 1,a	Green, Philip. DEADLY LOGIC: THE THEORY OF NUCLEAR DETERRENCE. Columbus: Ohio State University Press, 1966.
ARMS 1,4,b I. POLITICAL 1	Greenwood, Ted, Harold A. Feiveson, and Theodore B. Taylor. NUCLEAR PROLIFERATION: MOTIVATIONS, CAPABILITIES, AND STRATEGIES FOR CONTROL. New York: McGraw-Hill, 1977.
NONVIOLENCE 1,4,a	Gregg, Richard B. THE POWER OF NONVIOLENCE. New York: Schocken Books, 1966.
NONVIOLENCE 1,7	Gregg, Richard B. THE PSYCHOLOGY AND STRATEGY OF GANDHI'S NONVIOLENT RESISTANCE. New York: Garland, 1971 (Orig. pub. in India, 1929).

ATTITUDES a EDUCATION b	Griffith, Priscilla, and Betty Reardon. LET US EXAMINE OUR ATTITUDE TOWARD PEACE. Culver City, Calif.: Social Studies School Series, 1972.
CONFLICT 2 VIOLENCE 2,5	Grimshaw, Allen Day. RACIAL VIOLENCE IN THE UNITED STATES. Chicago: Aldine, 1969.
TERRORISM 2,4	Gross, Feliks. VIOLENCE IN POLITICS. The Hague: Mouton, 1972.
I. POLITICAL 1	Gross, Feliks. WORLD POLITICS AND TENSION AREAS. New York: New York University Press, 1966.
I. LAW 1,d	Grotius, Hugo. PROLEGOMENA TO THE LAW OF WAR AND PEACE. Indianapolis: Bobbs-Merrill, 1957 (Orig. pub., 1625).
I. POLITICAL 1,e	Guetzkow, Harold S., Chadwick F. Alger, Richard A. Brady, Robert Noel, and Richard C. Snyder. SIMULATION IN INTERNATIONAL RELATIONS: DEVELOPMENTS FOR RESEARCH AND TEACHING. Englewood Cliffs, N.J.: Prentice-Hall, 1963.
LIBERATION 1,b,c WARFARE c	Guevara, Che. THE DIARY OF CHE GUEVARA. New York: Bantam Books, 1967.
CONFLICT 1	Gumplowicz, Ludwig. THE OUTLINES OF SOCIOLOGY. Translated by Frederick W. Moore. Philadelphia: American Academy of Political and Social Science, 1899.

DEVELOPMENT 4,6, b,c I. ECONOMIC 4 I. POLITICAL 6 TRANSNATIONAL 6	Gunnemann, Jon P., Editor. THE NATION-STATE AND TRANS-NATIONAL CORPORATIONS IN CONFLICT: WITH SPECIAL REFER-ENCE TO LATIN AMERICA. New York: Praeger, in cooperation with the Council on Religion and International Affairs, 1975.
VIOLENCE 1	Gurr, Ted Robert. "A Compara-tive Study of Civil Strife," in Hugh Davis Graham and Ted Robert Gurr, Editors, VIO-LENCE IN AMERICA: HISTORICAL AND COMPARATIVE PERSPECTIVES. New York: Bantam Books, 1969.
CONFLICT 1 LIBERATION 1 VIOLENCE 1,4,7	Gurr, Ted Robert. WHY MEN REBEL. Princeton, N.J.: Princeton University Press, 1970.
	Gurr, Ted Robert, see Feierabend, Ivo K.
CONFLICT 4 FUTURES 3 I. POLITICAL 1	Gurvitch, Georges. "A Socio-logical Analysis of Inter-national Tensions," in Hadley Cantril, Editor, TENSIONS THAT CAUSE WARS. Urbana: University of Illinois Press, 1950.
INTEGRATION a I. ORGANIZATION 1,2,a TRANSNATIONAL a	Haas, Ernst B. BEYOND THE NATION STATE: FUNCTIONALISM AND INTERNATIONAL ORGANIZA-TION. Stanford, Calif.: Stanford University Press, 1964.
INTEGRATION b	Haas, Ernst B. HUMAN RIGHTS AND INTERNATIONAL ACTION: THE CASE OF FREEDOM OF ASSOCIA-TION. Stanford, Calif.: Stanford University Press, 1970.

CONFLICT 1,2,3 I. POLITICAL 1, 2,3	Haas, Michael. INTERNATIONAL CONFLICT. New York: Bobbs-Merrill, 1974.
CONFLICT 1 I. POLITICAL 1	Haas, Michael, Editor. INTERNATIONAL SYSTEMS: A BEHAVIORAL APPROACH. New York: Chandler, 1974.
EDUCATION 1,2,a,b, c,d	Haavelsrud, Magnus, Editor. EDUCATION FOR PEACE: REFLECTION AND ACTION. Guildford, Surrey, England: IPC Science and Technology Press, 1976.
I. ECONOMIC 4 TRANSNATIONAL 4,6	Haendel, Dan. FOREIGN INVESTMENTS AND THE MANAGEMENT OF POLITICAL RISK. Boulder, Colo.: Westview, 1978.
I. POLITICAL 2,a	Halberstam, David. THE BEST AND THE BRIGHTEST. New York: Random House, 1972.
	Hall, David K., see George, Alexander L.
INTEGRATION 1 TRANSNATIONAL 5	Hall, Edward T., and William Foote Whyte. "Inter-cultural Communication: A Guide to Men of Action." HUMAN ORGANIZATION, 19 (Spring 1960), 5-12.
CONFLICT 7	Hammond, Kenneth R., et al. "A Comparison of Cognitive Conflict Between Persons in Western Europe and the United States." INTERNATIONAL JOURNAL OF PSYCHOLOGY, 3, 1 (1968), 1-12.
CONFLICT 7 MEDIATION a RESEARCH b	Hammond, Kenneth R. "New Directions in Research on Conflict Resolution." JOURNAL OF SOCIAL ISSUES, 21, 3 (1965), 44-55.

CONFLICT 1,2 I. POLITICAL a	Hammond, Kenneth R., and Berndt Brehmer. "Quasi-rationality and Distrust Implications for International Conflict," in Leon Rappoport and David A. Summers, Editors, HUMAN JUDGMENT AND SOCIAL INTERACTION. New York: Holt, Rinehart and Winston, 1973.
	Hansford, Earle A., <u>see</u> Shure, Gerald H.
	Harbert, Joseph R., <u>see</u> Finger, Seymour Maxwell.
MEDIATION b MILITARY b	Harbottle, Michael. THE IMPARTIAL SOLDIER. London: Oxford University Press, 1970.
	Harbottle, Michael, <u>see</u> Rikhye, Indar Jit.
NONVIOLENCE 1,2, 5,7	Hare, A. Paul, Andrew Effrat, and Wyatt MacGaffey, Issue Editors. "Analysis of Nonviolence in Theory and Fact." SOCIOLOGICAL INQUIRY, 38, 1 (Winter 1968).
LIBERATION 1,5,b NONVIOLENCE 1,a	Hare, A. Paul, and Herbert H. Blumberg. LIBERATION WITHOUT VIOLENCE: A THIRD PARTY APPROACH. London: Rex Collings, 1977.
NONVIOLENCE 1,2, 7,c PROTEST 2	Hare, A. Paul, and Herbert H. Blumberg. NONVIOLENT DIRECT ACTION, AMERICAN CASES: SOCIAL PSYCHOLOGICAL ANALYSIS. Washington, D.C.: Corpus B Books, 1970.
	Hare, A. Paul, <u>see</u> Cooper, William.

ARMS 1,2,4,6
DEVELOPMENT 4,6
I. POLITICAL 1,2,6

Harkavy, Robert E. THE ARMS TRADE AND INTERNATIONAL SYSTEMS. Cambridge, Mass.: Ballinger, 1975.

MILITARY 1,4

Harries-Jenkins, Gwyn, and Jacques Van Doorn, Editors. THE MILITARY AND THE PROBLEM OF LEGITIMACY. Beverly Hills, Calif.: Sage, 1976.

FUTURES 1
I. POLITICAL 1

Harris, Errol E. ANNIHILATION AND UTOPIA: THE PRINCIPLES OF INTERNATIONAL POLITICS. London: Allen and Unwin, 1966.

Harris, Marvin, see Fried, Morton.

WARFARE 1,2

Harrison, Robert. WARFARE. Minneapolis: Burgess, 1973.

Hasenpflug, Hajo, see Sauvant, Karl P.

I. ORGANIZATION 2

Hazzard, Shirley. DEFEAT OF AN IDEAL: A STUDY OF THE SELF-DESTRUCTION OF THE UNITED NATIONS. Boston: Little, Brown, 1975.

Head, Richard G., see Short, Frisco W.

Heathcote, Nina, see Burns, Arthur L.

Hefner, Robert, see Kelman, Herbert C.

I. ECONOMIC 4
I. POLITICAL 6
RESOURCES b

Heinebäck, Bo. OIL AND SECURITY. New York: Humanities Press, 1974.

Heiss, Klaus P., see Morgenstern, Oskar.

I. POLITICAL 1

Held, Virginia. PHILOSOPHY, MORALITY AND INTERNATIONAL AFFAIRS. New York: Oxford University Press, 1974.

DEVELOPMENT 1,6,b I. ECONOMIC 1,4,a I. ORGANIZATION 1,2 I. POLITICAL 1,6 RESOURCES b TRANSNATIONAL 6	Helleiner, G., Editor. A WORLD DIVIDED: THE LESS DEVELOPED COUNTRIES IN THE INTERNATIONAL ECONOMY. New York: Cambridge University Press, 1976.
SECURITY a,b,f	Henkin, Louis. THE RIGHTS OF MAN TODAY. Boulder, Colo.: Westview, 1978.
	Herman, Theodore, see Beitz, Charles R.
CRISIS 1,2,3,7,b,c	Hermann, Charles F., Editor. INTERNATIONAL CRISES: INSIGHTS FROM BEHAVIORAL RESEARCH. New York: Free Press, 1973.
CRISIS 3,a RESEARCH b	Hermann, Charles F. RESEARCH TASKS FOR INTERNATIONAL CRISIS: AVOIDANCE AND MANAGEMENT. Columbus: Mershon Center, Ohio State University, 1975.
MILITARY 2,4	Herspring, Dale R., and Ivan Volgyes, Editors. CIVIL-MILITARY RELATIONS IN COMMUNIST SYSTEMS. Boulder, Colo.: Westview, 1978.
I. POLITICAL 1	Herz, John H. THE NATION-STATE AND THE CRISIS OF WORLD POLITICS: ESSAYS ON INTERNATIONAL POLITICS IN THE TWENTIETH CENTURY. New York: David McKay, 1976.
VIOLENCE 1,2,3,4,5,6,7	Hibbs, Douglas A., Jr. MASS POLITICAL VIOLENCE: A CROSS-NATIONAL CASUAL ANALYSIS. New York: Wiley, 1973.
	Hickie, John, see Elliot, R. S. P.

MILITARY 1,2	Hickman, Martin. THE MILITARY AND AMERICAN SOCIETY. Encino, Calif.: Glencoe Press, 1971.
MEDIATION 2,b MILITARY b	Higgins, Rosalyn. UNITED NATIONS PEACEKEEPING 1946-67: DOCUMENTS AND COMMENTARY. New York: Oxford University Press, 1970.
CRISIS 1,2 VIOLENCE a	Hilton, Gordon. "Expressions of Hostility in Crisis." JOURNAL OF PEACE RESEARCH, 3, 4 (1971), 249-262.
FUTURES 1,2,b	Hinsley, Francis H. POWER AND THE PURSUIT OF PEACE: THEORY AND PRACTICE IN THE HISTORY OF RELATIONS BETWEEN STATES. Cambridge, England: Cambridge University Press, 1963.
VIOLENCE 1,4,7,a	Hobbes, Thomas. LEVIATHAN. New York: Collier, 1962 (Orig. pub., 1651).
DEVELOPMENT c I. ECONOMIC 1,5 WARFARE 1	Hobson, John Atkinson. IMPERIALISM, A STUDY. Third Edition, revised. London: Allen and Unwin, 1938 (Orig. pub., 1902).
	Hoffenberg, Marvin, <u>see</u> Leontief, Wassily W.
WARFARE 1	Hoffman, Stanley. THE STATE OF WAR. New York: Praeger, 1965.
VIOLENCE 2	Hofstadter, Richard, and Michael Wallace. AMERICAN VIOLENCE: A DOCUMENTARY HISTORY. New York: Knopf, 1970.
	Hokanson, Jack E., <u>see</u> Megargee, Edwin I.
I. ORGANIZATION 1,a	Holcombe, Arthur N. A STRATEGY OF PEACE IN A CHANGING WORLD. Cambridge, Mass.: Harvard University Press, 1967.

FUTURES 1,3,b I. LAW 2	Hollins, Elizabeth Jay, Editor. PEACE IS POSSIBLE. New York: Grossman, 1966.
CRISIS 1 WARFARE 1	Holsti, Ole R. CRISIS, ESCALATION, WAR. Montreal: McGill-Queen's University Press, 1971.
	Holsti, Ole R., <u>see</u> North, Robert C.
CONFLICT 4,5 LIBERATION 4,5 NONVIOLENCE 4,5 PROTEST 4,5	Hope, Majorie. YOUTH AGAINST THE WORLD. Boston: Little, Brown, 1970.
	Hopmann, P. T., <u>see</u> Bobrow, Davis B.
TERRORISM 4,5,6 VIOLENCE 4,5	Horowitz, Irving Louis. GENOCIDE: STATE POWER AND MASS MURDER. New Brunswick, N.J.: Transaction Books, 1976.
MILITARY 1 RESEARCH c,d	Horowitz, Irving Louis. THE RISE AND FALL OF PROJECT CAMELOT. Cambridge, Mass.: MIT Press, 1967.
CONFLICT 1,2 DEVELOPMENT c	Horowitz, Irving Louis. THREE WORLDS OF DEVELOPMENT: THE THEORY AND PRACTICE OF INTERNATIONAL STRATIFICATION. Second Edition. New York: Oxford University Press, 1972 (Orig. pub., 1966).
CONFLICT 1 FUTURES 1 INTEGRATION 1 RESEARCH a WARFARE 1	Horowitz, Irving Louis. WAR AND PEACE IN CONTEMPORARY SOCIAL THEORY. New York: Humanities Press, 1974.
DEVELOPMENT 1,c DISARMAMENT 6 FUTURES 2 INTEGRATION 6 I. ECONOMIC 1	Hoselitz, Bert F., Editor. ECONOMICS AND THE IDEA OF MANKIND. New York: Columbia University Press, 1965.

I. POLITICAL 2,7,a	Howard, John R. FOURTEEN DECISIONS FOR UNDECLARED WAR. Washington, D.C.: University Press of America, 1978.
CONFLICT 1 DISARMAMENT 4,a I. POLITICAL 1 WARFARE 2	Howard, Michael. STUDIES IN WAR AND PEACE. New York: Viking, 1959.
WARFARE 1,2	Howard, Michael. WAR IN EUROPEAN HISTORY. London: Oxford University Press, 1976.
I. POLITICAL 1,a,e MEDIATION a	Howard, Nigel. PARADOXES OF RATIONALITY: THEORY OF METAGAMES AND POLITICAL BEHAVIOR. Cambridge, Mass.: MIT Press, 1971.
I. ECONOMIC 2,4 I. LAW 2	Hudec, Robert E. THE GATT LEGAL SYSTEM AND WORLD TRADE DIPLOMACY. New York: Praeger, 1975.
	Hudson, Michael C., <u>see</u> Taylor, Charles Davis.
INTEGRATION 1	Hughes, H. Stuart. APPROACH TO PEACE AND OTHER ESSAYS. New York: Atheneum, 1962.
	Hunter, Edna J., <u>see</u> McCubbin, Hamilton I.
MILITARY 1,4	Huntington, Samuel P. THE SOLDIER AND THE STATE. Cambridge, Mass.: Harvard University Press, 1957.
TERRORISM 1,4,a	Hutchinson, Martha Crenshaw. "The Concept of Revolutionary Terrorism." JOURNAL OF CONFLICT RESOLUTION, 16, 3 (September 1972), 383-396.
I. POLITICAL 2,a	Hveem, Helge. INTERNATIONAL RELATIONS AND WORLD IMAGES. Oslo: Universitetsforlaget, 1972.

I. ECONOMIC 1,4,a I. POLITICAL a,b,d RESOURCES 4,6,b	Hveem, Helge. THE POLITICAL ECONOMY OF THIRD WORLD PRODUCER ASSOCIATIONS: ON CONDITIONS AND CONSTRAINTS FOR EFFECTIVE COLLECTIVE ACTION AMONG RAW MATERIAL PRODUCING-EXPORTING COUNTRIES. Oslo: Universitetsforlaget, 1977.
DEVELOPMENT 1,b,c	Hveem, Helig. "The Global Dominance System: Notes on a Theory of Global Political Economy." JOURNAL OF PEACE RESEARCH, 4 (1973), 319-340.
TERRORISM 1	Hyam, E. TERRORISTS AND TERRORISM. London: J. M. Dent, 1975.
MEDIATION a WARFARE 1	Iklé, Fred C. EVERY WAR MUST END. New York: Columbia University Press, 1971.
MEDIATION a,e	Iklé, Fred C. HOW NATIONS NEGOTIATE. New York: Harper and Row, 1964.
EDUCATION b	Institute for World Order. PEACE AND WORLD ORDER STUDIES: A CURRICULUM GUIDE. New York: Institute for World Order, 1978.
I. POLITICAL 2,c	Institute of International Sociology, Gorizia. BOUNDARIES AND REGIONS: EXPLORATIONS IN THE GROWTH AND PEACE POTENTIAL OF THE PERIPHERIES. Trieste: Edizioni LINT, 1973.
I. ORGANIZATION 2 MEDIATION b MILITARY b	International Peace Academy. PEACEKEEPER'S HANDBOOK. New York: International Peace Academy, 1978.
INTEGRATION 1,4,a	INTERNATIONAL POLITICAL COMMUNITIES: AN ANTHOLOGY. New York: Doubleday, 1966.

CONFLICT 1,2,5,7
I. POLITICAL 1,7
WARFARE 1

International Sociological Association. THE NATURE OF CONFLICT: STUDIES ON THE SOCIOLOGICAL ASPECTS OF INTERNATIONAL TENSION. Paris: United Nations Educational, Scientific, and Cultural Organization, 1957.

DEVELOPMENT 3
DISARMAMENT 6
RESOURCES 3

Isard, Walter, and Stanislaw Czmanski. "A Model for the Projections of Industrial Structure, Land Use Patterns and Conversion Potentialities." PEACE RESEARCH SOCIETY (INTERNATIONAL) PAPERS, 5 (1966).

DISARMAMENT 1,a

Isard, Walter, and Phyllis Kaniss. "A Note on the Joint Use of GRIT and Veto-incremax Procedures," in Martin Pfaff, Editor, FRONTIERS OF SOCIAL THOUGHT: ESSAYS IN HONOR OF KENNETH E. BOULDING. New York: North-Holland, 1976.

EDUCATION 1,2
NONVIOLENCE 1,2

Ishitani, Susumu. "Nonviolent Action Training in Peace Education." PEACE RESEARCH IN JAPAN (1977-1978), 53-59.

MEDIATION 1,2,a

Jackson, Elmore. MEETING OF MINDS: A WAY TO PEACE THROUGH MEDIATION. New York: McGraw-Hill, 1952.

Jackson, Robert, see Corbet, Hugh.

INTEGRATION 4

Jacob, Philip, and James V. Toscano, Editors. THE INTEGRATION OF POLITICAL COMMUNITIES. Philadelphia: J. B. Lippincott, 1964.

CONFLICT 4
MILITARY 4,b

James, Alan. THE POLITICS OF PEACEKEEPING. New York: Praeger, 1969.

CONFLICT 1 WARFARE 1	James, William. THE MORAL EQUIVALENT OF WAR AND OTHER ESSAYS. Edited by John K. Roth. New York: Harper and Row, 1971.
CONFLICT 1,2,3,5,7	Jandt, Fred E. CONFLICT RESOLUTION THROUGH COMMUNICATION. New York: Harper and Row, 1973.
I. LAW c	Janis, Mark W. SEA POWER AND THE LAW OF THE SEA. Lexington, Mass.: D. C. Heath, 1976.
DEVELOPMENT 4 DISARMAMENT 5,a I. POLITICAL 1 MILITARY 1,2,4,5	Janowitz, Morris. MILITARY CONFLICT: ESSAYS IN THE INSTITUTIONAL ANALYSIS OF WAR AND PEACE. Beverly Hills, Calif.: Sage, 1975.
DEVELOPMENT 4 MILITARY 1,4,5,c	Janowitz, Morris. MILITARY INSTITUTIONS AND COERCION IN THE DEVELOPING NATIONS. Chicago: University of Chicago Press, 1977.
MILITARY 1,2,4,5,c	Janowitz, Morris. THE PROFESSIONAL SOLDIER: A SOCIAL AND POLITICAL PORTRAIT. Glencoe, Ill.: Free Press, 1960.
MILITARY 1,2,5	Janowitz, Morris, and Roger Little. SOCIOLOGY AND THE MILITARY ESTABLISHMENT. Beverly Hills, Calif.: Sage, 1974.
I. LAW 1,a,d	Jenks, Clarence Wilfred. THE COMMON LAW OF MANKIND. London: Stevens, 1958.
I. ORGANIZATION 1,2	Jenks, Clarence Wilfred. THE WORLD BEYOND THE CHARTER IN HISTORICAL PERSPECTIVE: A TENTATIVE SYNTHESIS OF FOUR STAGES OF WORLD ORGANIZATION. London: Rustin House, 1967.
	Jenks, Clarence Wilfred, <u>see</u> Larson, Arthur.

CONFLICT 3,f	Jensen, Lloyd. "Predicting International Events." PEACE RESEARCH REVIEWS, 4, 6 (August 1972).
ATTITUDES 4 I. POLITICAL 7	Jervis, Robert. PERCEPTIONS AND MISPERCEPTIONS IN INTERNATIONAL POLITICS. Princeton, N.J.: Princeton University Press, 1976.
I. ORGANIZATION 1 MEDIATION b	Johansen, Robert C., and Saul H. Mendlovitz. "Global Enforcement of the Just Law: A Proposal for a Transnational Police Force." FORUM, 8 (October 1976), 117-129.
FUTURES 1,b I. POLITICAL 1 NONVIOLENCE a SECURITY e	Johansen, Robert C. TOWARD A DEPENDABLE PEACE: A PROPOSAL FOR AN APPROPRIATE SECURITY SYSTEM. New York: Institute for World Order, 1978.
WARFARE c	Johnson, Chalmers. REVOLUTIONARY CHANGE. Boston: Little, Brown, 1966.
CONFLICT 7 MEDIATION 1,2	Johnson, D., and R. Duston. "The Initiation of Cooperation Through Role Reversal." JOURNAL OF SOCIAL PSYCHOLOGY, 82 (Second Half) (December 1970), 193-204.
WARFARE 1	Johnson, James Turner. IDEOLOGY, REASON, AND THE LIMITATIONS OF WAR: RELIGIOUS AND SECULAR CONCEPTS 1299-1740. Princeton, N.J.: Princeton University Press, 1975.
I. ORGANIZATION 2,a I. POLITICAL b,d	Jordan, Robert S. POLITICAL LEADERSHIP IN NATO: A STUDY IN MULTINATIONAL DIPLOMACY. Boulder, Colo.: Westview, 1978.
	Jordan, Robert S., see Weiss, Thomas G.

ATTITUDES 5,b I. POLITICAL 5	Joseph, Saud, and Barbara L. K. Pillsbury, Editors. MUSLIM-CHRISTIAN CONFLICT: ECONOMIC, POLITICAL, AND SOCIAL ORIGINS. Boulder, Colo.: Westview, 1978.
TRANSNATIONAL 1,3, 4,5	Judge, Anthony J. N. "The World Network of Organizations." INTERNATIONAL ASSOCIATIONS, 1 (1972), 18-25.
ATTITUDES c EDUCATION 1,2,a, b,f	Judson, Stephanie, Editor. A MANUAL ON NONVIOLENCE AND CHILDREN. Philadelphia: Nonviolence and Children Program, Friends Peace Committee, 1976.
FUTURES 1,3,b	Jungk, Robert, and Johan Galtung. MANKIND 2000. Oslo: Universitetsforlaget, 1969.
FUTURES 1 WARFARE 1	Kahn, Herman. THINKING ABOUT THE UNTHINKABLE. New York: Horizon, 1965.
FUTURES 1,3 I. POLITICAL 1	Kahn, Herman, and Anthony J. Wiener. THE YEAR 2000: A FRAMEWORK FOR SPECULATION ON THE NEXT THIRTY-THREE YEARS. Introduction by Daniel Bell. New York: Macmillan, 1967.
CONFLICT 1,2	Kahn, Robert L., and Elise Boulding, Editors. POWER AND CONFLICT IN ORGANIZATIONS. New York: Basic Books, 1964.
	Kaldor, Mary, <u>see</u> Elliott, Dave.
DISARMAMENT 1 RESEARCH a	Kaliadin, A. N. "Problems of Disarmament Research." JOURNAL OF PEACE RESEARCH, 3 (1972), 237-246.
	Kallab, Valeriana, <u>see</u> Erb, Guy, F.

DEVELOPMENT 1,2,b I. ORGANIZATION 1,2	Kamrany, Nake M., Editor. THE NEW ECONOMICS OF THE LESS DEVELOPED COUNTRIES: CHANGING PERCEPTIONS IN THE NORTH-SOUTH DIALOGUE. Boulder, Colo.: Westview, 1978.
DEVELOPMENT 1,2, 6,b I. ECONOMIC 2 I. POLITICAL 2	Kanet, Roger E., and Donna Bahry, Editors. SOVIET ECONOMIC AND POLITICAL RELATIONS WITH THE DEVELOPING WORLD. New York: Praeger, 1975.
	Kaniss, Phyllis, see Isard, Walter.
FUTURES 1 PROTEST 2	Kant, Immanuel. PERPETUAL PEACE: A PHILOSOPHIC ESSAY. Translated with notes by M. Campbell Smith; introduction by Robert Latta. New York: Garland, 1971 (Orig. pub., 1795). Also in Peter Mayer, Editor, THE PACIFIST CONSCIENCE, 1966.
I. LAW 1	Kaplan, Morton A., and Nicholas de B. Katzenbach. POLITICAL FOUNDATIONS OF INTERNATIONAL LAW. New York: Wiley, 1961.
CONFLICT 1,b I. POLITICAL 1,a, b,d	Kaplan, Morton A. SYSTEM AND PROCESS IN INTERNATIONAL POLITICS. New York: Wiley, 1957.
I. POLITICAL 1 WARFARE 1	Kára, Karl. "On the Marxist Theory of War and Peace." JOURNAL OF PEACE RESEARCH, 5, 1 (1968), 1-27.
	Katz, Elihu, see Crain, Robert.
	Katzenbach, Nicholas de B., see Kaplan, Morton A.
VIOLENCE 1,3	Kaufmann, Harry. AGGRESSION AND ALTRUISM: A PSYCHOLOGICAL ANALYSIS. New York: Holt, Rinehart and Winston, 1970.

	Kay, David A., see Goodrich, Leland M.
	Keen, James, see Oliver, Donald W.
MILITARY 2,4	Kelleher, Catherine, Editor. POLITICAL-MILITARY SYSTEMS: COMPARATIVE PERSPECTIVES. Beverly Hills, Calif.: Sage, 1974.
ATTITUDES 4 I. POLITICAL 1,a WARFARE 1,c	Kelly, George A., and Linda B. Miller. INTERNAL WAR AND INTERNATIONAL SYSTEMS: PERSPECTIVES ON METHOD. Cambridge, Mass.: Harvard University Press, 1969.
INTEGRATION 5	Kelman, Herbert C., and Raphael S. Ezkiel. CROSS NATIONAL ENCOUNTERS. San Francisco: Jossey-Bass, 1970.
ATTITUDES 4 INTEGRATION 4,7	Kelman, Herbert C., Editor. INTERNATIONAL BEHAVIOR: A SOCIAL-PSYCHOLOGICAL ANALYSIS. New York: Holt, Rinehart and Winston, 1965.
RESEARCH a	Kelman, Herbert C., William Barth, and Robert Hefner, Editors. "Research Approaches to the Study of War and Peace." JOURNAL OF SOCIAL ISSUES, 11, 1 (1955).
	Kelman, Herbert C., see Cohen, Stephen P.
I. LAW 1	Kelsen, Hans. "The Strategy of Peace." AMERICAN JOURNAL OF SOCIOLOGY, 46 (1941), 571-581; and 49 (1943), 381-389.
	Kemp, Geoffrey, see Ra'anan, Uri.

DISARMAMENT 6 MILITARY 1,6	Kemp, Jack, and Les Aspin. HOW MUCH DEFENSE SPENDING IS ENOUGH? Washington, D.C.: American Enterprise Institute for Public Policy Research, 1976.
WARFARE 2	Kende, Istvan. "Twenty-five Years of Local Wars." JOURNAL OF PEACE RESEARCH, 8, 1 (1971), 5-22.
DEVELOPMENT 2,3, 6,a MILITARY 2,6,c	Kennedy, Gavin. THE ECONOMICS OF DEFENCE. London: Faber and Faber, 1975.
ARMS 6 DEVELOPMENT 3,6 I. ECONOMIC 4 MILITARY 3,4,5,6 VIOLENCE 2 WARFARE 6	Kennedy, Gavin. THE MILITARY IN THE THIRD WORLD. London: Duckworth, 1974.
RESEARCH b,c,d	Kent, George. "The Application of Peace Studies." JOURNAL OF CONFLICT RESOLUTION, 15, 1 (March 1971), 47-53.
CONFLICT 1,2 I. POLITICAL a	Kent, George. THE EFFECTS OF THREATS. Columbus: Ohio State University Press, for the Mershon Center, 1967.
I. ECONOMIC 4 I. LAW c I. POLITICAL 1,2,6	Keohane, Robert O., and Joseph S. Nye, Jr. POWER AND INTERDEPENDENCE: WORLD POLITICS IN TRANSITION. Boston: Little, Brown, 1977.
DEVELOPMENT 4,6 I. ECONOMIC 2,4 I. LAW c I. POLITICAL 1,6 LIBERATION 6 TRANSNATIONAL 1,2, 4,6,b	Keohane, Robert O., and Joseph S. Nye, Jr., Editors. TRANSNATIONAL RELATIONS AND WORLD POLITICS. Cambridge, Mass.: Harvard University Press, 1971.
I. LAW 1,2 WARFARE 1,2	Khadduri, Majid. THE ISLAMIC LAW OF NATIONS. Baltimore: Johns Hopkins Press, 1966.

I. LAW 1,2
WARFARE 1,2 — Khadduri, Majid. WAR AND PEACE IN THE LAW OF ISLAM. Revised Edition. Baltimore: Johns Hopkins Press, 1962. (First Edition, 1955; orig. pub. under different title, 1940).

Khairov, Rustem, see Barsegov, Yuri.

FUTURES 1
I. POLITICAL 1 — Khrushchev, Nikita A. ON PEACEFUL CO-EXISTENCE: A COLLECTION BY KHRUSHCHEV. Moscow: Foreign Languages Publishing House, 1961.

CONFLICT 1
EDUCATION b — King, David C. PATTERNS OF HUMAN CONFLICT. Pleasantville, N.Y.: Schloat Productions, 1973.

NONVIOLENCE 1,2 — King, Martin Luther. STRIDE TOWARD FREEDOM. New York: Ballantine, 1961.

ARMS RACE 2
CIVILIAN DEF 1,6 — King-Hall, Stephen. DEFENSE IN THE NUCLEAR AGE. Nyack, N.Y.: Fellowship Publications, 1959.

I. POLITICAL a
WARFARE a — Kintner, William R. PEACE AND THE STRATEGY CONFLICT. New York: Praeger, 1967.

CONFLICT 1,2
EDUCATION a — Kirkland, Olin. ON CONFLICT: A CURRICULUM UNIT WITH COMMENTS. Orinda, Calif.: Diablo Valley Education Project, 1970.

Kirkpatrick, Kenneth, see Northwood, L. K.

I. POLITICAL a
WARFARE 1,a — Kissinger, Henry. NUCLEAR WEAPONS AND FOREIGN POLICY. New York: Norton, 1969.

ARMS 2
TERRORISM e
WARFARE 2,b,c — Klare, Michael T. WAR WITHOUT END: AMERICAN PLANNING FOR THE NEXT VIETNAMS. New York: Knopf, 1972.

I. POLITICAL 1,3	Klausner, Samuel, Editor. THE STUDY OF TOTAL SOCIETIES. Garden City, N.J.: Anchor Books, 1967.
ATTITUDES 4	Klineberg, Otto. THE HUMAN DIMENSIONS IN INTERNATIONAL RELATIONS. New York: Holt, Rinehart and Winston, 1964.
RESEARCH a	Kluckholm, Clyde. "Anthropological Research and World Peace," in APPROACHES TO WORLD PEACE. Proceedings of the 4th Conference on Science, Philosophy, and Religion in Their Relation to the Democratic Way of Life, New York, 1944. Millwood, N.Y.: Kraus Reprints, 1944.
I. POLITICAL a MEDIATION a	Knight, Douglas, H. W. Curtis, and Lawrence J. Fogel, Editors. CYBERNETICS, SIMULATION AND CONFLICT RESOLUTION. New York: Spartan, 1970.
MILITARY 4	Knoll, Erwin, and Judith McFadden, Editors. AMERICAN MILITARISM 1970. Epilogue by J. William Fulbright. New York: Viking, 1969.
WARFARE a	Knorr, Klaus. ON THE USES OF MILITARY POWER IN THE NUCLEAR AGE. Princeton, N.J.: Princeton University Press, 1966.
DEVELOPMENT c I. ECONOMIC 4 I. POLITICAL 6	Knorr, Klaus. THE POWER OF NATIONS: THE POLITICAL ECONOMY OF INTERNATIONAL RELATIONS. New York: Basic Books, 1975.
	Knorr, Klaus, <u>see</u> Morgenstern, Oskar.

CONFLICT 4 WARFARE 3	Köhler, Gernot. EVENTS RESEARCH AND WAR/PEACE PREDICTION. Oakville, Ontario: Canadian Peace Research Institute, 1974.
I. POLITICAL 2,a	Kolko, Gabriel. THE ROOTS OF AMERICAN FOREIGN POLICY. Boston: Beacon, 1971.
CONFLICT 5,7	Komorita, S., and M. Barnes. "Effects of Pressures to Reach Agreement in Bargaining." JOURNAL OF PERSONALITY AND SOCIAL PSYCHOLOGY, 13, 3 (November 1969), 245-252.
FUTURES 1,5	Kothari, Rajni. FOOTSTEPS INTO THE FUTURE: DIAGNOSIS OF THE PRESENT WORLD AND A DESIGN FOR AN ALTERNATIVE. New York: Free Press, 1976.
I. LAW 2	Kotzsch, Lothar. THE CONCEPT OF WAR IN CONTEMPORARY HISTORY AND INTERNATIONAL LAW. Geneva: Droz, 1956.
I. POLITICAL 1,2,7	Kratochwil, Friedrich V. INTERNATIONAL ORDER AND FOREIGN POLICY: A THEORETICAL SKETCH OF POST-WAR INTERNATIONAL POLITICS. Boulder, Colo.: Westview, 1978.
	Krause, Lawrence B., <u>see</u> Bergsten, C. Fred.
ATTITUDES 5 I. POLITICAL 7	Krieger, David. "A Note on the Consensus of International Relations Among American School Children." JOURNAL OF PEACE RESEARCH, 3 and 4 (1971), 305-306.
TRANSNATIONAL 1, 3,b	Kriesberg, Louis. "Centralization and Differentiation in International Nongovernmental Organizations." SOCIOLOGY AND SOCIAL RESEARCH, 61, 1 (October 1976), 1-23.

I. POLITICAL a	Kriesberg, Louis. "International Decisionmaking," in Michael Haas, et al., INTERNATIONAL SYSTEMS: A BEHAVIORAL APPROACH. New York: Chandler, 1974.
INTEGRATION 2,4 TRANSNATIONAL b	Kriesberg, Louis. "International Nongovernmental Organizations and Transnational Integration." INTERNATIONAL ASSOCIATIONS, 11 (November 1972), 520-525.
CONFLICT b I. POLITICAL e	Kriesberg, Louis, Editor. SOCIAL PROCESSES IN INTERNATIONAL RELATIONS. New York: Wiley, 1968.
CONFLICT 1,5	Kriesberg, Louis. SOCIOLOGY OF SOCIAL CONFLICTS. Englewood, Cliffs, N.J.: Prentice-Hall, 1973.
I. ORGANIZATION 1 I. POLITICAL 1 RESEARCH a TRANSNATIONAL 1	Kriesberg, Louis. "The State of the Discipline: Applied Sociology and International Relations." SOCIOLOGICAL PRACTICE, 1, 2 (Fall 1976), 116-131.
	Kritzer, Herbert M, see Lipsitz, Lewis.
DISARMAMENT 6	Kropotkin, Peter. THE CONQUEST OF BREAD. New York: New York University Press, 1972.
INTEGRATION 7 VIOLENCE b	Kropotkin, Peter. MUTUAL AID. Boston: Porter Sargent, 1955.
CONFLICT 1	Kuhn, Harold W., Issue Editor. "Game Theory, Bargaining, and International Relations." JOURNAL OF CONFLICT RESOLUTION, 6, 1 (March 1962).
RESEARCH a	Kumar, Mahendra. CURRENT PEACE RESEARCH AND INDIA. Rajghat, Varanasi, India: Gandhian Institute of Studies, 1968.

CONFLICT 1,2,5
I. POLITICAL 5
NONVIOLENCE 1

Kuper, Leo. RACE, CLASS AND POWER: IDEOLOGY AND REVOLUTIONARY CHANGE IN PLURAL SOCIETIES. London: Gerald Duckworth, 1974.

Kurth, James R., <u>see</u> Rosen, Steven J.

CONFLICT 2,5

Lacoutre, Jean. VIETNAM: BETWEEN TWO TRUCES. New York: Vintage Books, 1966.

TRANSNATIONAL 2,4,6,b

Ladon-Lederer, J. J. INTERNATIONAL NON-GOVERNMENTAL ORGANIZATIONS. Leyden, The Netherlands: A. W. Sythoff-Leyden, 1963.

FUTURES b

Lagos, Gustavo, and Horacio H. Godoy. REVOLUTION OF BEING: A LATIN AMERICAN VIEW OF THE FUTURE. New York: Free Press, 1977.

EDUCATION b

Lakewood Public Schools. A CURRICULUM TO HELP STUDENTS DEAL WITH FRUSTRATION AND AGGRESSION. Lakewood, Ohio: Lakewood Public Schools, 1971.

NONVIOLENCE 2,7

Lakey, George R. "The Sociological Mechanisms of Non-Violent Action." PEACE RESEARCH REVIEWS, 2, 6 (December 1968).

NONVIOLENCE 1
PROTEST 1

Lakey, George R. STRATEGY FOR A LIVING REVOLUTION. San Francisco: Freeman, 1973.

Lakey, George R., <u>see</u> Oppenheimer, Martin.

CONFLICT 1,2
MEDIATION 1,2

Lall, Arthur. MODERN INTERNATIONAL NEGOTIATION: PRINCIPLES AND PRACTICE. New York: Columbia University Press, 1966.

DISARMAMENT 1	Lall, Arthur. NEGOTIATING DISARMAMENT. Ithaca: Center for International Studies, Cornell University, 1964.
DISARMAMENT 6 RESEARCH a	Lall, Betty Goetz. PROSPERITY WITHOUT GUNS: THE ECONOMIC IMPACT OF REDUCTIONS IN DEFENSE SPENDING. New York: Institute for World Order, 1977.
	Lamb, W. Curtis, <u>see</u> Russett, Bruce M.
CONFLICT b INTEGRATION 4 I. LAW 1 I. POLITICAL e	Landheer, B., J. H. M. M. Loenen, Fred L. Polak. WORLD SOCIETY: HOW IS AN EFFECTIVE AND DESIRABLE WORLD ORDER POSSIBLE? A SYMPOSIUM. The Hague: Martinus Nijhoff, 1971.
MILITARY 1 RESEARCH a WARFARE 1	Lang, Jurt. MILITARY INSTITUTIONS AND THE SOCIOLOGY OF WAR: A REVIEW OF THE LITERATURE WITH ANNOTATED BIBLIOGRAPHY. Beverly Hills, Calif.: Sage, 1971.
LIBERATION 2,c WARFARE 2,c	Laqueur, Walter. GUERRILLA: A HISTORICAL AND CRITICAL STUDY. Boston: Little, Brown, 1976.
I. LAW 1,a	Larson, Arthur, and Clarence Wilfred Jenks. SOVEREIGNTY WITHIN THE LAW. New York: Oceana, 1965.
FUTURES 2	Larson, Arthur, Editor. A WARLESS WORLD. Foreword by U Thant. New York: McGraw-Hill, 1963.
VIOLENCE a	Larson, Otto N., Editor. VIOLENCE AND THE MASS MEDIA. New York: Harper, 1968.
	Larudee, Mehrene, <u>see</u> Pilisuk, Marc.

Lasswell, Harold D., see Lepawsky, Albert; Russett, Bruce M.

FUTURES b — Laszlo, Ervin. A STRATEGY FOR THE FUTURE: A SYSTEMS APPROACH TO WORLD ORDER. New York: Braziller, 1974.

ATTITUDES 1,2,3 — Laulicht, Jerome, and George W. Strong. THE CAUSES AND CORRELATES OF FORIEGN POLICY BELIEFS. Volumes I and II. Oakville, Ontario, Canada: Esperanto Press, 1963.

Laulicht, Jerome, see Paul, John; Rose, Peter I.

I. ECONOMIC 2 — Lauter, Geza P., and Paul M. Dickie. MULTINATIONAL CORPORATIONS AND EAST EUROPEAN SOCIALIST ECONOMICS. New York: Praeger, 1975.

EDUCATION 1,b — Lauter, Paul. TEACHING ABOUT PEACE ISSUES: A PEACE EDUCATION KIT. Philadelphia: American Friends Service Committee, 1965.

Lavipour, Farid G., see Sauvant, Karl P.

DISARMAMENT 1,2,a — Lawrence, Robert M. ARMS CONTROL AND DISARMAMENT: PRACTICE AND PROMISE. Minneapolis: Burgess, 1973.

Leeds, Anthony, see Vayda, Andrew P.

ARMS 1,a,b; DISARMAMENT 1,2,a; I. POLITICAL 1 — Legault, Albert, and George Lindsey. THE DYNAMICS OF THE NUCLEAR BALANCE. Ithaca, N.Y.: Cornell University Press, 1974.

MEDIATION b; MILITARY b — Legault, Albert. "Peace-Keeping Operations." PEACE RESEARCH REVIEWS, 2, 4 (1968).

ARMS 6 DISARMAMENT 6	Leitenberg, Milton. "The Conversion Potential of Military Research and Development Expenditures." BULLETIN OF PEACE PROPOSALS, 1 (1974), 73-87.
DEVELOPMENT 6,c RESOURCES 2,6,b	Leitenberg, Milton. "Notes on the Diversion of Resources for Military Purposes in Developing Nations." JOURNAL OF PEACE RESEARCH, 13, 2 (1976), 111-116.
ATTITUDES 4 CONFLICT 1 VIOLENCE 4 WARFARE c	Leites, Nathan, and Charles Wolf. REBELLION AND AUTHORITY. Chicago: Markham, 1970.
	Lengyel, Peter, *see* Makagiansar, Makaminan.
FUTURES b WARFARE c	Lenin, Vladimir I. LENIN ON WAR AND PEACE. Peking: Foreign Languages Press, 1966.
MILITARY 4	Lens, Sidney. THE MILITARY INDUSTRIAL COMPLEX. Philadelphia: Pilgrim, 1970.
RESEARCH b	Lentz, Theo F. TOWARDS A SCIENCE OF PEACE. New York: Bookman Associates, 1961 (Orig. pub., 1955).
	Lentz, Theo F., *see* Eckhardt, William.
DISARMAMENT 6	Leontief, Wassily W., and Marvin Hoffenberg. "The Economic Effects of Disarmament." SCIENTIFIC AMERICAN, 204, 4 (April 1961), 47-55; and 212, 4 (April 1965).
I. ECONOMIC 1,3,4	Leontief, Wassily W., *et al*. THE FUTURE OF THE WORLD ECONOMY. New York: Oxford University Press, 1977.

ARMS 4
INTEGRATION 1
I. LAW 1,2,d
I. POLITICAL 1,2, 5,a
SECURITY a

Lepawsky, Albert, Edward H. Buehrig, and Harold D. Lasswell, Editors. THE SEARCH FOR WORLD ORDER: STUDIES BY STUDENTS AND COLLEAGUES OF QUINCY WRIGHT. New York: Appleton-Century-Crofts, 1971.

Levinson, Daniel J., see Adorno, Theodore W.

INTEGRATION 1

Levy, Marion J., Jr. MODERNIZATION AND THE STRUCTURE OF SOCIETIES: A SETTING FOR INTERNATIONAL AFFAIRS. Volumes 1 and 2. Princeton, N.J.: Princeton University Press, 1966.

CONFLICT 7

Lewin, Kurt. RESOLVING SOCIAL CONFLICTS: SELECTED PAPERS ON GROUP DYNAMICS. Edited by Gertrude Weiss Lewin. New York: Harper, 1948.

LIBERATION 2

Lewis, John Wilson, Editor. PEASANT REBELLION AND COMMUNIST REVOLUTION IN ASIA. Stanford, Calif.: Stanford University Press, 1974.

CONFLICT 5,7
VIOLENCE 5,7

Lewis, Robert A. "Socialization into National Violence: Familial Correlates of Hawkish Attitudes Toward War." JOURNAL OF MARRIAGE AND THE FAMILY, 33, 4 (November 1971), 699-708.

INTEGRATION 2
PROTEST 2

Libby, Frederick J. TO END WAR: THE STORY OF THE NATIONAL COUNCIL FOR PREVENTION OF WAR. Nyack, N.Y.: Fellowship Publications, 1969.

CRISIS 2
WARFARE a

Lifton, Robert J. DEATH IN LIFE: SURVIVORS OF HIROSHIMA. New York: Random House, 1967.

WARFARE 2	Lifton, Robert J. HOME FROM THE WAR: VIETNAM VETERANS--NEITHER VICTIMS NOR EXECUTIONERS. New York: Simon and Schuster, 1973.
ATTITUDES 1,7	Lifton, Robert J. THOUGHT REFORM AND THE PSYCHOLOGY OF TOTALISM. New York: Norton, 1961.
I. ECONOMIC a	Lillich, Richard B., Editor. ECONOMIC COERCION AND THE NEW INTERNATIONAL ECONOMIC ORDER. Charlottesville, N.C.: Michie, 1976.
	Lindsey, George, <u>see</u> Legault, Albert.
CONFLICT 1,5 MEDIATION 1 RESEARCH a	Lipsitz, Lewis, and Herbert M. Kritzer. "Unconventional Approaches to Conflict Resolution: Erikson and Sharp on Non-Violence." JOURNAL OF CONFLICT RESOLUTION, 19, 4 (December 1975), 713-733.
	Liske, Craig, <u>see</u> Raichur, Satish.
DEVELOPMENT 4 MILITARY 1,2	Lissak, Moshe. MILITARY ROLES IN MODERNIZATION: CIVIL-MILITARY RELATIONS IN THAILAND AND BURMA. Beverly Hills, Calif.: Sage, 1976.
WARFARE b,c	Littauer, Rapheal, and Norman Uphoff, Editors. THE AIR WAR IN INDOCHINA. Revised Edition. Boston: Beacon, 1972.
	Little, Roger, <u>see</u> Janowitz, Morris.
	Lloyd, Georgia, <u>see</u> Wynner, Edith.

DEVELOPMENT 1,2,4, 5,6	Loehr, William, and John P. Powelson, Editors. ECONOMIC DEVELOPMENT, POVERTY, AND INCOME DISTRIBUTION. Boulder, Colo.: Westview, 1977.
	Loenen, J. H. M. M., see Landheer, B.
CONFLICT 1,5,7 MEDIATION 1	Loomis, Charles P. "In Praise of Conflict and its Resolution." AMERICAN SOCIOLOGICAL REVIEW, 6, 32 (December 1967), 875-890.
INTEGRATION 2	Loomis, J. L. "Communication, the Development of Trust and Cooperative Behavior." HUMAN RELATIONS, 12 (1959).
EDUCATION b,c I. ECONOMIC 4 I. POLITICAL 6	Lopez, George A. DEPENDENCE AND INTERDEPENDENCE IN THE INTERNATIONAL SYSTEM: AN INTRODUCTION TO INTERNATIONAL POLITICAL ECONOMY. Columbus: Consortium for International Studies Education, Ohio State University, 1978.
	Lopez, George A., see Garrigan, Timothy B.
ATTITUDES 1,5 INTEGRATION 1,5,7 I. POLITICAL 1,2, a,b,d MEDIATION b MILITARY 1,2,7,b WARFARE 1,2	Lopez-Reyes, Ramon. POWER AND IMMORTALITY: ESSAYS ON STRATEGY, WAR PSYCHOLOGY AND WAR CONTROL. New York: Exposition, 1971.
VIOLENCE 7,b	Lorenz, Konrad. ON AGGRESSION. Translated by Marjorie Kerr Wilson. New York: Harcourt, Brace and World, 1966.
INTEGRATION 1	Lovell, John P. THE SEARCH FOR PEACE: AN APPRAISAL OF ALTERNATIVE APPROACHES. Pittsburgh: International Studies Association, 1974.

DISARMAMENT 1,a INTEGRATION 4 I. ORGANIZATION 1 I. POLITICAL 1,b	Luard, David Evan Trant. CONFLICT AND PEACE IN THE MODERN INTERNATIONAL SYSTEM. Boston: Little, Brown, 1968 (Orig. pub., 1962 as PEACE AND OPINION).
I. ORGANIZATION 1,2 I. POLITICAL c	Luard, David Evan Trant, Editor. INTERNATIONAL REGULATION OF FRONTIER DISPUTES. New York: Praeger, 1970.
I. POLITICAL 1,2,5	Luard, David Evan Trant. TYPES OF INTERNATIONAL SOCIETY. Oxford, England: Oxford University Press, 1976.
CONFLICT 1 I. POLITICAL a,e	Luce, R. Duncan, and Howard Raiffa. GAMES AND DECISIONS: INTRODUCTION AND CRITICAL SURVEY. New York: Wiley, 1958.
	Lugo, Ariel E., see Van Raay, Hans G. T.
	Lunde, Walter, see Sorokin, Pitirim.
VIOLENCE 4,a	Lupsha, Peter. "Explanation of Political Violence: Some Psychological Theories Versus Indignation." POLITICS AND SOCIETY, 2 (Fall 1971).
WARFARE c	Lutz, William, and Harry Brent, Editors. ON REVOLUTION. Cambridge, Mass.: Winthrop, 1971.
NONVIOLENCE 2	Lynd, Staughton, Editor. NONVIOLENCE IN AMERICA: A DOCUMENTARY HISTORY. Indianapolis: Bobbs-Merrill, 1966.
RESEARCH a VIOLENCE 7,a	Lystad, Mary Hanemann. "Violence at Home: A Review of the Literature." AMERICAN JOURNAL OF ORTHOPSYCHIATRY, 45, 3 (April 1975), 328-345.

RESEARCH b	McClelland, Charles A. "The Function of Theory in International Relations." JOURNAL OF CONFLICT RESOLUTION, 4, 3 (September 1960), 303-336.
ATTITUDES 5,c I. POLITICAL 1,7	McClelland, David C. POWER: THE INNER EXPERIENCE. New York: Halsted, 1975.
MILITARY 5,7	McCubbin, Hamilton I., Barbara B. Dahl, and Edna J. Hunter, Editors. FAMILIES IN THE MILITARY SYSTEM. Beverly Hills, Calif.: Sage, 1976.
	MacDougall, John A., see Evan, William M.
	McFadden, Judith, see Knoll, Erwin.
	McFarlane, Robert C., see Short, Frisco W.
	MacGaffey, Wyatt, see Hare, A. Paul.
FUTURES 1,b I. ECONOMIC 4 RESOURCES 4,d	MacGillis, Miariam Therese, and Gerald Mische. "Hunger and World Order." WHOLE EARTH PAPERS, 1, 3 (1977).
EDUCATION 1,b	McGinnis, James B. A STRATEGY GUIDE FOR SCHOOLS AND SCHOOL SYSTEMS IN EDUCATION FOR PEACE AND JUSTICE. St. Louis: Institute for Education in Peace and Justice, 1977.
	McGinnis, James B., see McGinnis, Kathy.

EDUCATION b,c

McGinnis, Kathy, James B. McGinnis, Mary Ann McGivern, and Luanne Schinzel. EDUCATING FOR PEACE AND JUSTICE: A MANUAL FOR TEACHERS. Fifth Edition. St. Louis: Institute for Education in Peace and Justice, 1976.

McGivern, Mary Ann, see McGinnis, Kathy.

FUTURES 1

McHale, John. THE FUTURE OF THE FUTURE. New York: Braziller, 1969.

WARFARE 1

Machiavelli, Niccolo. THE ARTS OF WAR. Indianapolis: Bobbs-Merrill, 1965.

I. POLITICAL 1,2

MacIver, Robert M. THE NATIONS AND THE UNITED NATIONS. Prepared for the Carnegie Endowment for International Peace to summarize a series of studies: National Studies on International Organization. New York: Manhattan, 1959.

WARFARE 1

MacIver, Robert M. ON COMMUNITY, SOCIETY AND POWER: SELECTED WRITINGS. Edited by Leon Bramson. Chicago: University of Chicago Press, 1970.

Mack, Andrew, see Boserup, Anders.

CONFLICT 1
RESEARCH a

Mack, Raymond, and Richard Snyder. "The Analysis of Social Conflict--Toward an Overview and Synthesis." JOURNAL OF CONFLICT RESOLUTION, 1, 2 (June 1957), 212-248. Also in Amitai Etzioni and Martin Wenglinsky, Editors, WAR AND ITS PREVENTION; and in Clagett G. Smith, Editor, CONFLICT RESOLUTION.

EDUCATION 1,b,c
NONVIOLENCE c

McKay, Bidge. TRAINING FOR NON-VIOLENT ACTION FOR HIGH SCHOOL STUDENTS: A HANDBOOK. Philadelphia: Friends Peace Committee, 1971.

TERRORISM 7

McKnight, Gerald. THE TERRORIST MIND: WHY THEY HIJACK, KIDNAP, BOMB AND KILL. New York: Bobbs-Merrill, 1975.

I. LAW 2
I. ECONOMIC 4

McMillan, Carl H., Editor. CHANGING PERSPECTIVES IN EAST-WEST COMMERCE. Lexington, Mass.: Lexington Books, 1974.

CONFLICT 1,2
VIOLENCE 5

McNeil, Elton B., Editor. THE NATURE OF HUMAN CONFLICT. Englewood Cliffs, N.J.: Prentice-Hall, 1965.

CONFLICT 1
VIOLENCE b
WARFARE 1

McNeill, William H. PLAGUES AND PEOPLES. Garden City, N.Y.: Anchor Books, 1976.

RESEARCH b
VIOLENCE 1,2

Makagiansar, Makaminan, and Peter Lengyel, Issue Editors. "The Scientific Bases of Peace." IMPACT OF SCIENCE ON SOCIETY, 18, 2 (April-June 1968).

DEVELOPMENT 4,6

Mallon, Richard D., and Juan V. Sourrouille. ECONOMIC POLICYMAKING IN A CONFLICT SOCIETY: THE ARGENTINE CASES. Cambridge, Mass.: Harvard University Press, 1975.

CONFLICT 1,2,7
DISARMAMENT 2
I. POLITICAL 2

Mandel, Robert. PERCEPTION, DECISION MAKING, AND CONFLICT. Washington, D.C.: University Press of America, 1978.

Mankind 2000, see Union of International Associations.

WARFARE 1	Mannheim, Karl. MAN AND SOCIETY IN AN AGE OF RECONSTRUCTION. New York: Harcourt, Brace, 1950.
WARFARE c	Mao Tse Tung. ON PROTRACTED WAR. Peking: Foreign Languages Press, 1967.
INTEGRATION 1	Mark, Max. BEYOND SOVEREIGNTY. Washington, D.C.: Public Affairs Press, 1965.
DEVELOPMENT 1,7,b I. ECONOMIC 4,a	Mark, Max. "The Domestic and International Quest for Economic Equality--The Interaction Process." INTERNATIONAL INTERACTIONS, 4, 2 (1978).
ATTITUDES a DEVELOPMENT 7	Mark, Max. MODERN IDEOLOGIES. New York: St. Martin's, 1973.
NONVIOLENCE 2,5	Martin, David A. PACIFISM: AN HISTORICAL AND SOCIOLOGICAL STUDY. New York: Schocken Books, 1965.
ARMS 4 I. POLITICAL 1	Marwah, Ankar, and Ann Schulz, Editors. NUCLEAR PROLIFERATION AND THE NEAR-NUCLEAR COUNTRIES. Cambridge, Mass.: Ballinger, 1976.
ATTITUDES 3 INTEGRATION 3,7	Marwell, Gerald, and David R. Schmitt. COOPERATION: AN EXPERIMENTAL ANALYSIS. New York: Academic, 1975.
WARFARE 5	Marwick, Arthur. WAR AND SOCIAL CHANGE IN THE TWENTIETH CENTURY. New York: St. Martin's, 1975.
	Marx, Karl. For works about Marx, see Kára, Karl; Pomeroy, William.

ATTITUDES 1 INTEGRATION 1	Matter, Joseph Allen. LOVE, ALTRUISM, AND WORLD CRISIS: THE CHALLENGE OF PITIRIM SOROKIN. Chicago: Nelson-Hall, 1974.
VIOLENCE 7,b	May, Rollo. POWER AND INNOCENCE: A SEARCH FOR THE SOURCES OF VIOLENCE. New York: Norton, 1972.
	May, William H., see Osgood, Charles E.
NONVIOLENCE a,b	Mayer, Peter, Editor. THE PACIFIST CONSCIENCE. Chicago: Holt, Rinehart, and Winston, 1966.
	Maynard, Charles, see Northwood, L, K.
TRANSNATIONAL b	Maza, Herbert. NEUF MENEURS INTERNATIONAUX: DE L'INITIATIVE INDIVIDUELLE DANS L'INSTITUTION DES ORGANIXATIONS INTERNATIONAL PENDANT LE XIXe ET LES XXe SIECLE. Paris: Cirey, 1965.
FUTURES 1,2 I. ECONOMIC 1 I. POLITICAL 1,d	Mazrui, Ali A., and Hasu H. Patel, Editors. AFRICA IN WORLD AFFAIRS: THE NEXT THIRTY YEARS. New York: Third Press, 1973.
I. ECONOMIC 2 I. POLITICAL 2,d RESOURCES a	Mazrui, Ali A. AFRICA'S INTERNATIONAL RELATIONS: THE DIPLOMACY OF DEPENDENCY AND CHANGE. Boulder, Colo.: Westview, 1978.
FUTURES b	Mazrui, Ali A. A WORLD FEDERATION OF CULTURES: AN AFRICAN PERSPECTIVE. New York: Free Press, 1976.
CONFLICT 2 INTEGRATION 2	Mead, Margaret. COOPERATION AND COMPETITION AMONG PRIMITIVE PEOPLES. New York: McGraw-Hill, 1967.

	Meeker, Robert J., <u>see</u> Shure, Gerlad H.
VIOLENCE 1,2,7,b	Megargee, Edwin I., and Jack E. Hokanson, Editors. THE DYNAMICS OF AGGRESSION: INDIVIDUAL, GROUP, AND INTERNATIONAL ANALYSES. New York: Harper and Row, 1970.
CONFLICT 2 INTEGRATION 2	Melko, Matthew. 52 PEACEFUL SOCIETIES. Ontario: Canadian Peace Research Institute, 1973.
DISARMAMENT 6	Melman, Seymour, Editor. THE DEFENSE ECONOMY: CONVERSION OF INDUSTRIES AND OCCUPATIONS TO CIVILIAN NEEDS. New York: Praeger, 1970.
ARMS 1 DISARMAMENT 1,b INTEGRATION 1	Melman, Seymour. THE PEACE RACE. New York: Ballantine Books, 1961.
DISARMAMENT 6 MILITARY 1,2,4,6	Melman, Seymour. PENTAGON CAPITALISM: THE POLITICAL ECONOMY OF WAR. New York: McGraw-Hill, 1970.
ARMS 2,6 MILITARY 2,4,6	Melman, Seymour. THE PERMANENT WAR ECONOMY: AMERICAN CAPITALISM IN DECLINE. New York: Simon and Schuster, 1974.
FUTURES b TRANSNATIONAL 1,4	Mendlovitz, Saul H., Editor. ON THE CREATION OF A JUST WORLD ORDER: PREFERRED WORLDS FOR THE 1990s. New York: Free Press, 1975.
	Mendlovitz, Saul H., <u>see</u> Falk, Richard A.; Johansen, Robert C.
DEVELOPMENT 1,5,6 INTEGRATION 1 I. ORGANIZATION 1 I. POLITICAL 1	Menegazzi, Guido. LAWS AND MODELS FOR A VITAL ORDER AND MUTUAL DEVELOPMENT OF PEOPLES. Verona, Italy: Palazzo Giuliari, 1975.

INTEGRATION 1,6 TRANSNATIONAL 1,3, 4,6	Mennis, Bernhard, and Karl P. Sauvant. EMERGING FORMS OF TRANSNATIONAL COMMUNITY: TRANSNATIONAL ENTERPRISES AND REGIONAL INTEGRATION. Lexington, Mass.: Lexington Books, 1976.
	Merrill, John C., see Fischer, Heintz-Dietrich.
	Messer, Sylvia, see Dreachslin, Janice.
PROTEST 2,3,7	Michener, James P. KENT STATE: WHAT HAPPENED AND WHY. New York: Random House, 1971.
DEVELOPMENT 1,4 I. ORGANIZATION 1,2,3 I. POLITICAL 1,2, 3,b MEDIATION 2,3 VIOLENCE 1 WARFARE 1,2,3,a, b,c	Midlarsky, Manus I. ON WAR: POLITICAL VIOLENCE IN THE INTERNATIONAL SYSTEM. New York: Free Press, 1975.
CRISIS 2 VIOLENCE 5	Midlarsky, Manus I. "Power, Uncertainty, and the Onset of International Violence." JOURNAL OF CONFLICT RESOLUTION, 18, 3 (September 1974).
RESOURCES 4	Mikdashi, Zuhayr. THE INTERNATIONAL POLITICS OF NATURAL RESOURCES. Ithaca, N.Y.: Cornell University Press, 1976.
	Milburn, Thomas W., see Bonoma, Thomas V.
VIOLENCE 7	Milgram, Stanley. OBEDIENCE TO AUTHORITY. New York: Harper and Row, 1974.

DEVELOPMENT 4,5,6 EDUCATION b	Millar, Jayne C. FOCUSING ON GLOBAL POVERTY AND DEVELOPMENT: A RESOURCE BOOK FOR EDUCATORS. Washington, D.C.: Overseas Development Council, 1974.
	Miller, Frederick D., see Cohen, Stephen P.
	Miller, Linda B., see Kelly, George A.
	Miller, N. E., see Dollard, John.
I. POLITICAL 2	Miller, Welbert C. INTERNATIONAL COMMUNITY POWER STRUCTURES: COMPARATIVE STUDIES OF FOUR WORLD CITIES. Bloomington: Indiana University Press, 1970.
NONVIOLENCE 1,2, a,b	Miller, William Robert. NONVIOLENCE. London: Allen and Unwin, 1965.
DISARMAMENT 1,2 FUTURES 6	Millis, Walter, and James Real. THE ABOLITION OF WAR. New York: Macmillan, 1963.
WARFARE 1,2	Millis, Walter. ARMS AND MEN. New York: Putnam, 1956.
DISARMAMENT b FUTURES 1,3 I. LAW a	Millis, Walter. AN END TO ARMS. New York: Atheneum, 1965.
MILITARY 4	Mills, C. Wright. THE CAUSES OF WORLD WAR III. New York: Oxford University Press, 1959.
MILITARY 1,2	Mills, C. Wright. THE POWER ELITE. New York: Oxford University Press, 1956.
NONVIOLENCE a	Milne, A. A. PEACE WITH HONOUR. New York: E. P. Dutton, 1934.

I. POLITICAL e WARFARE 2,3	Milstein, Jeffrey S. DYNAMICS OF THE VIETNAM WAR: A QUANTITATIVE ANALYSIS AND PREDICTIVE COMPUTER SIMULATION. Columbus: Ohio State University Press, 1974.
	Miron, Murray S., <u>see</u> Osgood, Charles E.
ARMS 1,2,4,5 FUTURES 1,b I. ECONOMIC 1,2, 4,5	Mische, Gerald, and Patricia Mische. TOWARD A HUMAN WORLD ORDER: BEYOND THE NATIONAL SECURITY STRAITJACKET. New York: Paulist Press, 1977.
	Mische, Gerald, <u>see</u> MacGillis, Miariam Therese.
ARMS 5 ATTITUDES 5,c	Mische, Patricia. "A Cloud Over Family Life." SIGN MAGAZINE (May 1977).
FUTURES 1	Mische, Patricia. "Human Future: Finding a Basis for Hope." DAWNPOINT MAGAZINE (Association for Humanistic Psychology) (Winter 1978).
ARMS 5 EDUCATION a,b RESOURCES 1,d,f	Mische, Patricia. "Parenting in a Hungry World." NEW CATHOLIC WORLD (November 1977).
DISARMAMENT 2,5	Mische, Patricia, Issue Editor. "Women and Disarmament." WHOLE EARTH PAPERS, 1, 7 (1978).
CONFLICT 4 FUTURES b	Mische, Patricia. "Women and Power." WHOLE EARTH PAPERS, 1, 8 (1978).
DISARMAMENT 5 I. POLITICAL 5	Mische, Patricia. "Women and World Order." WHOLE EARTH PAPERS, 1, 8 (1978).
	Mische, Patricia, <u>see</u> Mische, Gerald.

INTEGRATION a
I. ORGANIZATION 1

Mitrany, David. THE FUNCTIONAL THEORY OF POLITICS. New York: St. Martin's, 1976.

FUTURES b

Mitrany, David. A WORKING PEACE SYSTEM. Chicago: Quadrangle Books, 1966.

TRANSNATIONAL 6

Modelski, George, Editor. MULTINATIONAL CORPORATIONS AND WORLD ORDER. Beverly Hills, Calif.: Sage, 1974.

Modigliani, Andre, see Gamson, William A.

VIOLENCE 7

Montagu, Ashley, Editor. MAN AND AGGRESSION. Second Edition. New York: Oxford University Press, 1973 (Orig. pub., 1968).

ATTITUDES a
EDUCATION 1
VIOLENCE 7

Montessori, Maria. EDUCATION AND PEACE. Translated by Helen R. Lane. Chicago: Henry Regnery, 1972.(Orig. pub., 1949).

Moore, Christopher, see Coover, Virginia.

I. POLITICAL 1

Moore, Wilbert E. "Global Sociology: The World as a Singular System." AMERICAN JOURNAL OF SOCIOLOGY, 5 (March 1966), 475-482.

PROTEST 7

Morgan, William. "Faculty Mediation of Student War Protests," in Foster and Long, Editors, STUDENT PROTEST IN AMERICA. Clifton, N.J.: Morrow, 1972.

DEVELOPMENT 3
I. POLITICAL 3
MILITARY 3

Morgenstern, Oskar, Klaus Knorr, and Klaus P. Heiss. LONG TERM PROJECTIONS OF POWER: POLITICAL, ECONOMIC, AND MILITARY FORECASTING. Cambridge, Mass.: Ballinger, 1973.

I. POLITICAL 1,2, 3,a	Morgenthau, Hans J. POLITICS AMONG NATIONS. New York: Knopf, 1967.
VIOLENCE b	Morris, Desmond. THE HUMAN ZOO. New York: McGraw-Hill, 1969.
I. ORGANIZATION 2	Morris, Roger, and Hal Sheets. DISASTER IN THE DESERT: FAILURES OF INTERNATIONAL RELIEF IN THE WEST AFRICAN DROUGHT. Washington, D.C.: Carnegie Endowment for International Peace, 1974.
MILITARY 2	Moskos, Charles C. THE AMERICAN ENLISTED MAN: RANK AND FILE IN TODAY'S MILITARY. New York: Russell Sage Foundation, 1970.
MILITARY 1,4	Moskos, Charles C. "The Concept of the Military-Industrial Complex: Radical Critique or Liberal Bogey?" SOCIAL PROBLEMS, 21, 4 (Spring 1974), 498-512.
MILITARY 5	Moskos, Charles C. "The Military." ANNUAL REVIEW OF SOCIOLOGY, 2 (1976), 55-77.
ATTITUDES 2 MEDIATION 2,b MILITARY 2,b	Moskos, Charles C. PEACE SOLDIERS: THE SOCIOLOGY OF A UNITED NATIONS MILITARY FORCE. Chicago: University of Chicago Press, 1976.
ATTITUDES 1,5 MILITARY 5	Moskos, Charles C., Editor. PUBLIC OPINION AND THE MILITARY ESTABLISHMENT. Beverly Hills, Calif.: Sage, 1971.
INTEGRATION b I. LAW 2	Moskowitz, Moses. INTERNATIONAL CONCERN WITH HUMAN RIGHTS. Leyden, The Netherlands: A. W. Sitjhoff, 1974.
TERRORISM 2,a	Moss, Robert. THE WAR FOR THE CITIES. New York: Coward McCann and Geoghegan, 1972.

Mott, William C., see Barnett, Frank R.

Mowrer, A. H., see Dollard, John.

CONFLICT 1
EDUCATION 1
TRANSNATIONAL 1,2
Mudd, Stuart, Editor. CONFLICT RESOLUTION AND WORLD EDUCATION. The Hague: Dr. W. Junk, 1966.

Mukerjee, Tapan, see Boulding, Kenneth E.

Müller, Ronald E., see Barnett, Richard J.

ATTITUDES a
CONFLICT 1,2,7
Muney, Barbara, and Morton Deutsch. "The Effects of Role-Reversal During the Discussion of Opposing Viewpoints." JOURNAL OF CONFLICT RESOLUTION, 12, 3 (September 1968), 345-356.

ATTITUDES 5
CONFLICT 7
Murphy, Gardner, Editor. HUMAN NATURE AND ENDURING PEACE; THIRD YEARBOOK OF THE SOCIETY FOR THE PSYCHOLOGICAL STUDY OF SOCIAL ISSUES. Boston: Houghton Mifflin, 1945.

Murphy, Robert, see Fried, Morton.

WARFARE c
Mus, Paul. VIETNAM: SOCIOLOGIE D'UNE GUERRE. Paris: Editions du Seuil, 1952.

NONVIOLENCE 1,a,b
Muste, A. J. NONVIOLENCE IN AN AGGRESSIVE WORLD. New York: Harper, 1940.

MILITARY 2,5,7
Myer, Samuel, and Albert D. Biderman, Editors. MASS BEHAVIOR IN BATTLE AND CAPTIVITY. Chicago: University of Chicago Press, 1968.

ARMS 4
DISARMAMENT 4,a

Myrdal, Alva. THE GAME OF DISARMAMENT: HOW THE UNITED STATES AND RUSSIA RUN THE ARMS RACE. New York: Pantheon, 1976.

DEVELOPMENT c
RESOURCES a,b

Myrdal, Gunnar. ASIAN DRAMA: AN INQUIRY INTO THE POVERTY OF NATIONS. 3 volumes. New York: Pantheon, 1968.

DEVELOPMENT c
RESOURCES a,b

Myrdal, Gunnar. THE CHALLENGE OF WORLD POVERTY: A WORLD POVERTY PROGRAM OUTLINE. New York: Pantheon, 1970.

NONVIOLENCE 2
RESOURCES a,b,c

Nader, Ralph, and Donald Ross. ACTION FOR CHANGE: A STUDENT'S MANUAL FOR PUBLIC INTEREST ORGANIZING. New York: Viking, 1972.

NONVIOLENCE 1,2, a,b

Naess, Arne. GANDHI AND GROUP CONFLICT: AN EXPLORATION OF SATYAGRAHA: THEORETICAL BACKGROUND. Oslo: Universitetsforlaget, 1974.

NONVIOLENCE 2

Naess, Arne. "A Systematization of Gandhian Ethics of Conflict Resolution." JOURNAL OF CONFLICT RESOLUTION, 2, 2 (June 1958), 140-155.

ATTITUDES 2

Nakamura, Hajime. WAYS OF THINKING OF EASTERN PEOPLES. Honolulu: East-West Center Press, 1964.

CONFLICT 1,g

Nardin, Terry. "Theories of Conflict Management." PEACE RESEARCH REVIEWS, 4, 2 (April 1971).

Naroll, Frada, <u>see</u> Naroll, Raoul.

ARMS 2,a	Naroll, Raoul, Vern L. Bullough, and Frada Naroll. MILITARY DETERRENCE IN HISTORY: A PILOT CROSS-HISTORICAL SURVEY. Albany, N.Y.: State University of New York Press, 1974.
DISARMAMENT 6,b EDUCATION c MILITARY 2,6 RESEARCH e	National Action/Research on the Military Industrial Complex. HOW TO RESEARCH YOUR LOCAL WAR INDUSTRY. Philadelphia: American Friends Service Committee, 1973.
	Nef, John C., <u>see</u> Barnett, Frank R.
VIOLENCE 1,2,7 WARFARE 2	Nef, John U. WAR AND HUMAN PROGRESS: AN ESSAY ON THE RISE OF INDUSTRIAL CIVILIZATION. New York: Norton, 1963 (Orig. pub., 1950).
DEVELOPMENT 6,b TRANSNATIONAL 6	Negandhi, Anant R., and S. Benjamin Prasad. THE FRIGHTENING ANGELS: A STUDY OF U.S. MULTINATIONALS IN DEVELOPING NATIONS. Kent, Ohio: Kent State University Press, 1975.
EDUCATION b RESEARCH a	Nesbitt, William. TEACHING ABOUT WAR AND WAR PREVENTION. New York: Crowell, 1971.
EDUCATION c	Nesbitt, William, Norman Abramovitz, and Charles Bloomstein. TEACHING YOUTH ABOUT CONFLICT AND WAR. Washington, D.C.: National Council for the Social Studies, 1973.
	Nesvold, Betty, <u>see</u> Gillespie, J.
I. POLITICAL 1	Nettl, J. P., and Roland Robertson. INTERNATIONAL SYSTEMS AND THE FORMATION OF NATIONAL GOALS AND ATTITUDES. New York: Basic Books, 1968.

	Nettleship, Anderson, <u>see</u> Nettleship, Martin A.
WARFARE 1,3	Nettleship, Martin A., R. Dale Givens, and Anderson Nettleship, Editors. WAR, ITS CAUSES AND CORRELATES. The Hague: Mouton, 1975.
	Nettleship, Martin A., <u>see</u> Givens, R. Dale.
RESEARCH b	Newcombe, Alan G., Michael Wallace, Paul Smoker, and William Eckhardt. "Alternative Approaches to Peace Research." PEACE RESEARCH REVIEWS, 4, 4 (February 1972).
WARFARE 1,2,3	Newcombe, Alan G., and James Wert. AN INTER-NATION TENSIONMETER FOR THE PREDICTION OF WAR. Oakville, Ontario: Canadian Peace Research Institute, 1972.
	Newcombe, Alan G., <u>see</u> Newcombe, Hanna.
FUTURES 6 INTEGRATION 4	Newcombe, Hanna. "Alternative Approaches to World Government." PEACE RESEARCH REVIEWS, 5, 3 (February 1974).
RESEARCH a	Newcombe, Hanna. "Design for a Better World: Thirty-two Theses." PEACE RESEARCH, 8, 1 (1976), 1-6.
I. ORGANIZATION 3	Newcombe, Hanna. PATTERNS OF NATIONS: INTERACTIONS IN THE U.N. 1946-1971. Oakville, Ontario: Canadian Peace Research Institute, 1973.
RESEARCH a	Newcombe, Hanna, and Alan G. Newcombe. PEACE RESEARCH AROUND THE WORLD. Oakville, Ontario: Canadian Peace Research Institute, 1969.

	Newcombe, Hanna, <u>see</u> Waters, Judy.
ARMS a DISARMAMENT a	Newhouse, John. COLD DAWN: THE STORY OF SALT. New York: Holt, Rinehart and Winston, 1973.
ARMS 4 CONFLICT 1,3,b CRISIS 2 I. POLITICAL 6 RESEARCH b	Nicholson, Michael. CONFLICT ANALYSIS. London: English Universities Press, 1970.
VIOLENCE b WARFARE 1,2	Nicolai, G. F. THE BIOLOGY OF WAR. New York: Century, 1918.
VIOLENCE 4,7	Nieburg, H. L. POLITICAL VIOLENCE: THE BEHAVIORAL PROCESS. New York: St. Martin's, 1969.
ATTITUDES 1	Nietzsche, Friedrich. THE WILL TO POWER. New York: Vintage, 1968.
DISARMAMENT 2 I. POLITICAL 1 MILITARY b RESEARCH a	Niezing, Johan. SOCIOLOGY, WAR AND DISARMAMENT: STUDIES IN PEACE RESEARCH. Rotterdam: Rotterdam University Press, 1970.
LIBERATION c TERRORISM a WARFARE c	Niezing, Johan, Editor. URBAN GUERRILLA. Proceedings of the First International Working Conference on Violence and Non-Violent Action in Industrialized Societies, Brussels, March 13-15, 1974. Rotterdam: Rotterdam University Press, 1974.
CONFLICT 2 WARFARE 1,2,c	Nkrumah, Kwame. CHALLENGE OF THE CONGO: A CASE STUDY OF FOREIGN PRESSURES ON AN INDEPENDENT STATE. New York: International, 1967.
WARFARE c	Nkrumah, Kwame. HANDBOOK OF REVOLUTIONARY WARFARE. New York: International, 1968.

	Noel, Robert, <u>see</u> Guetzkow, Harold S.
DISARMAMENT 1	Noel-Baker, Philip J. DISARMAMENT. New York: Garland, 1971 (Orig. pub., 1926).
ATTITUDES 1	Nordskog, J. E. "Peace as a Revolutionary Ideal." SOCIOLOGY AND SOCIAL RESEARCH, 30, 1, 11-20.
MILITARY 4	North American Council on Latin America (NACLA). THE U.S. MILITARY APPARATUS. Berkeley, Calif.: North American Council on Latin America, 1972.
CRISIS 3	North, Robert C., Ole R. Holsti, M. George Zaninovich, and Dina A. Zinnes. CONTENT ANALYSIS: A HANDBOOK WITH APPLICATIONS FOR THE STUDY OF INTERNATIONAL CRISIS. Evanston, Ill.: Northwestern University Press, 1963.
	North, Robert C., <u>see</u> Choucri, Nazli.
INTEGRATION 1 I. LAW a WARFARE 2	Northrop, Filmer S. C. THE TAMING OF THE NATIONS. New York: Macmillan, 1953.
DISARMAMENT 6 MILITARY 1 NONVIOLENCE c	Northwood, Lawrence, K., Issue Editor, with Ann Blalock, Kenneth Kirkpatrick, and Charles Maynard. "Warfare or Welfare: Which Direction for America?" JOURNAL OF SOCIOLOGY AND SOCIAL WELFARE, 4, 3-4 (January/March, 1977).
DISARMAMENT 3,a	Novick, Sheldon. THE CARELESS ATOM. Boston: Houghton Mifflin, 1969.

I. POLITICAL a — Nuechterlein, Donald E. NATIONAL INTERESTS AND PRESIDENTIAL LEADERSHIP: THE SETTING OF PRIORITIES. Boulder, Colo.: Westview, 1978.

Nurock, Max, see Boasson, Charles.

I. ORGANIZATION a — Nye, Joseph S., Jr. PEACE IN PARTS: INTEGRATION AND CONFLICT IN REGIONAL ORGANIZATION. Boston: Little, Brown, 1971.

Nye, Joseph S., Jr., see Keohane, Robert O. (1971, 1977).

CONFLICT 5
PROTEST 5 — Oberschall, Anthony. SOCIAL CONFLICT AND SOCIAL MOVEMENTS. Englewood Cliffs, N.J.: Prentice-Hall, 1973.

NONVIOLENCE 1 — Ofshe, Richard. "The Effectiveness of Pacifist Strategies: A Theoretical Approach." JOURNAL OF CONFLICT RESOLUTION, 15, 2 (June 1971), 261-269.

CONFLICT 2
WARFARE 1,2 — Ogburn, William F., Editor. AMERICAN SOCIETY IN WARTIME. New York: DeCapo Printing, 1972 (Orig. pub., 1944).

INTEGRATION 4,5
I. POLITICAL d — O'Leary, James P. SYSTEMS THEORY AND REGIONAL INTEGRATION: THE "MARKET MODEL" OF INTERNATIONAL POLITICS. Washington, D.C.: University Press of America, 1978.

EDUCATION 1
INTEGRATION 1,2 — Oliver, Donald W., and James Keen. "Global Issues and Community." HISTORY AND SOCIAL SCIENCE TEACHER (Special issue in "Bringing the World into the Classroom"), 13, 4 (Summer 1978), 229-236.

	Olson, Theodore, see Cooper, William; Shivers, Lynn.
NONVIOLENCE 1,7,a PROTEST 2	Oppenheimer, Martin, and George Lakey. A MANUAL FOR DIRECT ACTION: STRATEGY AND TACTICS FOR CIVIL RIGHTS AND ALL OTHER NONVIOLENT PROTEST MOVEMENTS. Chicago: Quadrangle Books, 1965.
	Organski, A. F. K., see Organski, Katherine.
FUTURES 1	Organski, Katherine, and A. F. K. Organski. POPULATION AND WORLD POWER. New York: Knopf, 1961.
RESEARCH b	Orlans, Harold. "Ethical Problems in the Relations of Research Sponsors and Investigators," in Gideon Sjoberg, Editor, ETHICS, POLITICS AND SOCIAL RESEARCH. Cambridge, Mass.: Schenkman, 1967.
WARFARE c	Osanka, Franklin Mark, Editor. MODERN GUERRILLA WARFARE. New York: Free Press, 1962.
CONFLICT 7 I. POLITICAL a MEDIATION 1,a	Osgood, Charles E. AN ALTERNATIVE TO WAR OR SURRENDER. Urbana: University of Illinois Press, 1962.
ATTITUDES 1,2	Osgood, Charles E., William H. May, and Murray S. Miron. CROSS-CULTURAL UNIVERSALS OF AFFECTIVE MEANING. Urbana: University of Illinois Press, 1975.
CONFLICT 1 MEDIATION a	Osgood, Charles E. "Escalation and De-Escalation as Political Strategies." PHI KAPPA PHI JOURNAL, 47 (1947), 3ff.
VIOLENCE 5	Osgood, Robert E. FORCE, ORDER, AND JUSTICE. Baltimore: Johns Hopkins Press, 1967.

WARFARE b	Osgood, Robert E. LIMITED WAR: THE CHALLENGE TO AMERICAN STRATEGY. Chicago: University of Chicago Press, 1957.
EDUCATION 1 RESEARCH 2	OUR GENERATION AGAINST NUCLEAR WAR, "Supplement on Peace Research,"3, 2 (October 1964).
CONFLICT 5,d DEVELOPMENT 5	Paige, Jeffery M. AGRARIAN REVOLUTION: SOCIAL MOVEMENTS AND EXPORT AGRICULTURE IN THE UNDERDEVELOPED WORLD. New York: Free Press, 1975.
	Pannenborg, Charles O., <u>see</u> Akkerman, Robert J.
WARFARE 1,2	Park, Robert E. "The Social Function of War: Observations and Notes." AMERICAN JOURNAL OF SOCIOLOGY, 46 (1941), 551-570. Reprinted in Leon Bramson and George W. Goethals, Editors, WAR: STUDIES FROM PSYCHOLOGY, SOCIOLOGY, ANTHROPOLOGY.
VIOLENCE 7	Parsons, Talcott. "Certain Primary Sources and Patterns of Aggression in the Social Structure of the Western World," in Talcott Parsons, Editor, ESSAYS IN SOCIAL THEORY, PURE AND APPLIED. Glencoe, Ill.: Free Press, 1949.
	Patel, Hasu H., <u>see</u> Mazrui, Ali A.
PROTEST 2,b	Patterson, David S. TOWARD A WARLESS WORLD: THE TRAVAIL OF THE AMERICAN PEACE MOVEMENT 1887-1914. Bloomington: Indiana University Press, 1976.

ATTITUDES 3	Paul, John, Jerome Laulicht, and George Strong. IN YOUR OPINION: LEADERS' AND VOTERS' ATTITUDES ON DEFENSE AND DISARMAMENT. Oakville, Ontario: Canadian Peace Research Institute, 1968.
WARFARE 1,2,c	Paynton, Clifford T., and Robert Blackey. WHY REVOLUTION? THEORIES AND ANALYSES. Cambridge, Mass.: Schenkman, 1971. Distributed by General Learning Press, Morristown, N.J.
DEVELOPMENT 2 NONVIOLENCE a,b RESEARCH a,b WARFARE 1	PEACE RESEARCH FOR PEACE ACTION. Based on a seminar report; sponsored jointly by Gandhi Peace Foundation and Gandhian Institute of Studies. New Delhi: Indian Council of Peace Research, 1972.
ATTITUDES 7	Pear, T. H., Editor. PSYCHOLOGICAL FACTORS OF PEACE AND WAR. New York: Philosophical Library, 1950.
I. ECONOMIC 4 I. LAW c RESOURCES a	Pearson, Charles S. INTERNATIONAL MARINE ENVIRONMENT POLICY: THE ECONOMIC DIMENSIONS. Baltimore: Johns Hopkins Press, 1975.
MEDIATION a	Pechota, Vratislav. COMPLEMENTARY STRUCTURES OF THIRD-PARTY SETTLEMENT OF INTERNATIONAL DISPUTES. New York: United Nations Institute for Training and Research, 1971.
MEDIATION a	Pechota, Vratislav. THE QUIET APPROACH: A STUDY OF THE GOOD OFFICES EXERCISED BY THE UNITED NATIONS SECRETARY-GENERAL IN THE CAUSE OF PEACE. New York: United Nations Institute for Training and Research, 1972.

NONVIOLENCE 7 — Pelton, Leroy H. THE PSYCHOLOGY OF NONVIOLENCE. New York: Pergamon Press, 1974.

MILITARY 4 — Perruci, Robert, and Marc Pilisuk, Editors. THE TRIPLE REVOLUTION EMERGING: SOCIAL PROBLEMS IN DEPTH. Boston: Little, Brown, 1971.

Peters, Scott, <u>see</u> Waters, Judy.

CONFLICT 1; FUTURES 1; INTEGRATION 1; I. POLITICAL 1,7 — Pettman, Ralph. HUMAN BEHAVIOR AND WORLD POLITICS. New York: St. Martin's, 1975.

Pfaltzgraff, Robert L., Jr., <u>see</u> Ra'anan, Uri.

INTEGRATION 6,7 — Phelps, Edmund S., Editor. ALTRUISM, MORALITY, AND ECONOMIC THEORY. Beverly Hills, Calif.: Sage, 1975.

CONFLICT g — Phipps, Thomas. "Resolving 'Hopeless' Conflicts." JOURNAL OF CONFLICT RESOLUTION, 5, 3 (September 1961), 274-279.

I. POLITICAL 1 — Picht, Georg. "On the Concept of Peace." SOCIAL RESEARCH, 42, 1 (Spring 1975), 101-111.

CIVILIAN DEF 1,2; DEVELOPMENT 1,2; INTEGRATION 4; PROTEST 2,3 — Pickus, Robert, and Robert Woito. TO END WAR: AN INTRODUCTION, IDEAS, BOOK, ORGANIZATIONS, WORK THAT CAN HELP. Revised Edition. New York: Harper and Row, 1970.

ATTITUDES 1,3 — Pilisuk, Marc, and Paul Skolnick. "Inducing Trust: A Test of the Osgood Proposal." JOURNAL OF PERSONALITY AND SOCIAL PSYCHOLOGY, 8, 2 (Part I) (February 1968), 121-133.

DEVELOPMENT a,b
MILITARY 1,2,4 — Pilisuk, Marc, with the assistance of Mehrene Larudee. INTERNATIONAL CONFLICT AND SOCIAL POLICY. Englewood Cliffs, N.J.: Prentice-Hall, 1972.

Pilisuk, Marc, _see_ Perruci, Robert.

Pillsbury, Barbara L. K., _see_ Joseph, Saud.

RESOURCES a,b,c — Pirages, Dennis C., and Paul R. Ehrlich. ARK II: SOCIAL RESPONSE TO ENVIRONMENTAL IMPERATIVES. New York: Viking, 1974

FUTURES b
I. LAW a
I. ORGANIZATION 2 — Plano, Jack C., and Robert E. Riggs. FORGING WORLD ORDER: THE POLITICS OF INTERNATIONAL ORGANIZATION. New York: Macmillan, 1967.

I. POLITICAL 2,3,a — Plate, Thomas. UNDERSTANDING DOOMSDAY: A GUIDE TO THE ARMS RACE FOR HAWKS, DOVES AND PEOPLE. Foreword by Senator George McGovern. New York: Simon and Schuster, 1971.

ARMS 2,4 — Platt, Alan, and Lawrence D. Weiler, Editors. CONGRESS AND ARMS CONTROL. Boulder, Colo.: Westview, 1978.

ARMS 2,4 — Platt, Alan. THE U.S. SENATE AND STRATEGIC ARMS POLICY, 1969-1977. Boulder, Colo.: Westview, 1978.

Polak, Fred L., _see_ Landheer, B.

WARFARE c — Pomeroy, William, Editor. GUERRILLA WARFARE AND MARXISM. New York: International, 1970.

ATTITUDES 3 TRANSNATIONAL 5	Pool, Ithiel de Sola. "Effects of Cross-National Contact on the National and International Images," in Herbert C. Kelman, Editor, INTERNATIONAL BEHAVIOR. New York: Holt, Rinehart and Winston, 1965.
I. POLITICAL 2,5 TRANSNATIONAL 2,5	Pool, Ithiel de Sola. THE PRESTIGE PRESS: A COMPARATIVE STUDY OF POLITICAL SYMBOLS. Cambridge, Mass.: MIT Press, 1970.
ATTITUDES 1	Pool, Ithiel de Sola. SYMBOLS OF INTERNATIONALISM. Introduction by Quincy Wright. Stanford, Calif.: Stanford University Press, 1951.
ATTITUDES 3 CONFLICT 1	Powell, Elwin H. THE DESIGN OF DISCORD. New York: Oxford University Press, 1970.
	Powelson, John P., see Loehr, William.
	Prasad, S. Benjamin, see Negandhi, Anant R.
WARFARE 1,2	Preston, Richard A., Sydney Wise, and Herman Werner. MEN IN ARMS. New York: Praeger, 1962.
DISARMAMENT 2,a I. ORGANIZATION 2	Price, Charles C., and Louis B. Sohn. REPORT ON EVOLVING INTERNATIONAL INSTITUTIONS FOR ARMS LIMITATION AND DISARMAMENT. Arlington, Va.: World Federalists Association, 1977.
PROTEST 2 VIOLENCE 1,4,5,7,b WARFARE 1,a,c	Prosterman, Roy. SURVIVING TO 3000: AN INTRODUCTION TO THE STUDY OF LETHAL CONFLICT. North Scituate, Mass.: Duxbury Press, 1972.

INTEGRATION 4 — Proudhon, Pierre-Joseph. LA GUERRE ET LA PAIX: RECHERCHES SUR LE PRINCIPE ET LA CONSTITUTION DU DROIT DES GENS. New York: Garland, 1971 (Orig. pub. in Paris, 1861).

VIOLENCE 5 — Pruitt, Dean G., and Richard C. Snyder, Editors. THEORY AND RESEARCH ON THE CAUSES OF WAR. Englewood Cliffs, N.J.: Prentice-Hall, 1969.

ARMS 2 — Pugwash Symposium, Tenth. IMPACT OF NEW TECHNOLOGIES ON THE ARMS RACE. Proceedings of the 10th Pugwash Symposium held at Wingspread, Racine, Wisconsin, June 26-29, 1970. Cambridge, Mass.: MIT Press, 1971.

ARMS a; I. POLITICAL 2,3 — Quester, George. NUCLEAR DIPLOMACY: THE FIRST TWENTY-FIVE YEARS. Second Edition. New York: Dunellen, 1973.

ARMS 4,6; DEVELOPMENT 4,6,b — Ra'anan, Uri, Robert L. Pfaltzgraff, Jr., and Geoffrey Kemp, Editors. ARMS TRANSFERS TO THE THIRD WORLD: PROBLEMS AND POLICIES. Boulder, Colo.: Westview, 1978.

DEVELOPMENT 2,4,6, a,b; I. ECONOMIC 2,4; I. POLITICAL 2,6 — Raichur, Satish, and Craig Liske, Editors. THE POLITICS OF AID, TRADE AND INVESTMENT. New York: Russell Sage Foundation, 1976. Distributed by Wiley/Halsted.

Raiffa, Howard, <u>see</u> Luce, R. Duncan.

Ramers, Robert K., <u>see</u> Barringer, Richard E.

MEDIATION a,b WARFARE 1,2	Randle, Robert F. THE ORIGINS OF PEACE: A STUDY OF PEACE-MAKING AND THE STRUCTURE OF PEACE SETTLEMENTS. New York: Free Press, 1973.
CONFLICT 1,2,7 I. POLITICAL 1,2,7 MEDIATION a	Rapoport, Anatol. THE BIG TWO: SOVIET-AMERICAN PERCEPTIONS OF FOREIGN POLICY. New York: Bobbs-Merrill, 1971.
CONFLICT 1 VIOLENCE b	Rapoport, Anatol. CONFLICT IN A MAN-MADE ENVIRONMENT. Baltimore: Penguin Books, 1974.
CONFLICT 1	Rapoport, Anatol. FIGHTS, GAMES AND DEBATES. Ann Arbor: University of Michigan Press, 1960.
ARMS a DISARMAMENT 1,a I. POLITICAL e	Rapoport, Anatol. "Games Which Simulate Deterrence and Disarmament." PEACE RESEARCH REVIEWS, 1, 4 (August 1967).
CONFLICT 1,b	Rapoport, Anatol, and Albert M. Chammah. PRISONER'S DILEMMA: A STUDY IN CONFLICT AND COOPERATION. Ann Arbor: University of Michigan Press, 1965.
CONFLICT 1,b	Rapoport, Anatol. STRATEGY AND CONSCIENCE. New York: Harper, 1964.
CONFLICT 1,b INTEGRATION 1	Rapoport, Anatol. "Threat, Trade and Love," in Martin Pfaff, Editor, FRONTIERS IN SOCIAL THOUGHT: ESSAYS IN HONOR OF KENNETH BOULDING. New York: North-Holland, 1976.
	Rayman, Paula, <u>see</u> Bruyn, Severyn T.
	Real, James, <u>see</u> Millis, Walter.
	Reardon, Betty, <u>see</u> Griffith, Priscilla.

ATTITUDES 1,2 TRANSNATIONAL 5	Reigrotski, Erich, and Nels Anderson. "National Stereotypes and Foreign Contacts." PUBLIC OPINION QUARTERLY, 23 (Winter 1960), 515-528.
I. LAW 1	Reisman, W. Michael, and Burns H. Weston, Editors. TOWARD WORLD ORDER AND HUMAN DIGNITY: ESSAYS IN HONOR OF MYRES S. McDOUGAL. New York: Free Press, 1976.
DISARMAMENT a FUTURES 5,6,7 TRANSNATIONAL 5	Reves, Emery. ANATOMY OF PEACE. New York: Harper, 1945.
	Rhinelander, J. B., see Willrich, Mason.
I. POLITICAL 2,3 VIOLENCE 5	Richardson, Lewis F. ARMS AND INSECURITY: A MATHEMATICAL STUDY OF THE CAUSES AND ORIGINS OF WAR. Pittsburgh: Boxwood Press, 1960.
I. POLITICAL 3 WARFARE 3	Richardson, Lewis F. STATISTICS OF DEADLY QUARRELS. Pittsburgh: Boxwood Press, 1960.
EDUCATION a,b,d	Richardson, Robert, Editor. LEARNING FOR CHANGE IN WORLD SOCIETY: REFLECTIONS, ACTIVITIES AND RESOURCES. London: World Studies Project, 1976.
	Riggs, Robert E., see Plano, Jack C.
MEDIATION 2,b MILITARY 2,b	Rikhye, Indar Jit, Michael Harbottle, and Bjørn Egge. THE THIN BLUE LINE: INTERNATIONAL PEACEKEEPING AND ITS FUTURE. New Haven, Conn.: Yale University Press, 1974.

I. ORGANIZATION 1,2,4,5	Rittberger, Volker. EVOLUTION AND INTERNATIONAL ORGANIZATION: TOWARDS A NEW LEVEL OF SOCIOPOLITICAL INTEGRATION. The Hague: Martinus Nijhoff, 1973.
PROTEST 2	Robbins, Keith. THE ABOLITION OF WAR: THE "PEACE MOVEMENT" IN BRITAIN, 1914-1919. Cardiff: University of Wales Press, 1976.
CIVILIAN DEF 1	Roberts, Adam, Editor. CIVILIAN RESISTANCE AS A NATIONAL DEFENSE: NONVIOLENT RESISTANCE TO AGGRESSION. Baltimore: Penguin Books, 1969 (Orig. pub. in London, 1967, as STRATEGY OF CIVILIAN DEFENCE).
CIVILIAN DEF 1,2,b	Roberts, Adam. NATIONS IN ARMS: THE THEORY AND PRACTICE OF TERRITORIAL DEFENSE. New York: Praeger, for the International Institute for Strategic Studies, 1976.
	Robertson, Roland, see Nettl, J. P.
ATTITUDES 2 I. POLITICAL a	Robinson, James A., and Richard C. Snyder. "Decision-making in International Politics," in Herbert Kelman, Editor, INTERNATIONAL BEHAVIOR: A SOCIAL-PSYCHOLOGICAL ANALYSIS. New York: Holt, Rinehart and Winston, 1965.
ATTITUDES 3 I. POLITICAL a MEDIATION a	Rose, Peter I., and Jerome Laulicht, Issue Editors. "The Threat of War: Policy and Public Opinion." SOCIAL PROBLEMS, 11, 1 (Summer 1963).
ARMS 1,2,b I. LAW 1,2 WARFARE 2,a	Rose, Steven, Editor. CBW: CHEMICAL AND BIOLOGICAL WARFARE. Boston: Beacon, 1968.

ARMS 5 CONFLICT 1,e I. POLITICAL a MEDIATION a	Rosecrance, Richard, Editor. THE FUTURE OF THE INTER-NATIONAL STRATEGIC SYSTEM. San Francisco: Chandler, 1972.
VIOLENCE 7	Rosell, Leif. "Children's Views of War and Peace." JOURNAL OF PEACE RESEARCH, 5, 3 (1968), 268-276.
DEVELOPMENT 1,2,4, 6,b,c	Rosen, Steven J., and James R. Kurth, Editors. TESTING THEORIES OF ECONOMIC IMPERI-ALISM. Lexington, Mass.: D. C. Heath, 1974.
I. POLITICAL a	Rosenau, James N., Editor. COMPARING FOREIGN POLICIES: THEORIES, FINDINGS AND METHODS. Beverly Hills, Calif.: Sage, 1974.
I. POLITICAL 1	Rosenau, James N., Editor. IN SEARCH OF GLOBAL PATTERNS. New York: Free Press, 1976.
INTEGRATION 1 I. POLITICAL 1	Rosenau, James N., Editor. LINKAGE POLITICS: ESSAYS ON THE CONVERGENCE OF NATIONAL AND INTERNATIONAL SYSTEMS. New York: Free Press, 1969.
I. POLITICAL a	Rosenau, James N. SCIENTIFIC STUDY OF FOREIGN POLICY. New York: Free Press, 1971.
I. POLITICAL a	Rosenberg, Milton, Editor. BEYOND CONFLICT AND CONTAINMENT--CRITICAL STUDIES OF MILITARY AND FOREIGN POLICY--A READER. New Bruns-wick, N.J.: Transaction/ Society Books, 1972.
	Rosenthal, Donald, see Crain, Robert.
	Ross, Donald, see Nader, Ralph.

CONFLICT 1,3,7 INTEGRATION 1,3,7 MEDIATION 1,3,7	Rubin, Jeffrey Z., and Bert R. Brown. THE SOCIAL PSYCHOLOGY OF BARGAINING AND NEGOTIATION. New York: Academic Press, 1975.
DISARMAMENT 4,5 PROTEST 4	Rubin, Josephine. "Women and Peace." WHOLE EARTH PAPERS, 1, 6 (1978).
I. POLITICAL 1,2,3 TRANSNATIONAL 6	Rummel, Rudolph J. THE DIMENSIONS OF NATIONS. Beverly Hills, Calif.: Sage, 1972.
CONFLICT 7 WARFARE 7	Rummel, Rudolph J. UNDERSTANDING CONFLICT AND WAR. Volume 1: THE DYNAMIC PSYCHOLOGICAL FIELD. New York: Wiley, 1975.
CONFLICT 1,5	Rummel, Rudolph J. UNDERSTANDING CONFLICT AND WAR. Volume 2: THE CONFLICT HELIX. New York: Wiley, 1976.
NONVIOLENCE a WARFARE 1	Russell, Bertrand. JUSTICE IN WARTIME. New York: Garland, 1971 (Orig. pub. in London, 1917).
MEDIATION a VIOLENCE 5	Russell, Bertrand. WHY MEN FIGHT: A METHOD OF ABOLISHING THE INTERNATIONAL DUEL. New York: Garland, 1971 (Orig. pub., 1917).
LIBERATION 1,2,c WARFARE 1,2,c	Russell, D. E. H. REBELLION, REVOLUTION AND ARMED FORCE: A COMPARATIVE STUDY OF FIFTEEN COUNTRIES WITH SPECIAL EMPHASIS ON CUBA AND SOUTH AFRICA. New York: Academic Press, 1974.
RESEARCH b	Russett, Bruce M. "From Peace Research to Peace Action: Some Pertinent Ethical Questions." BULLETIN OF PEACE PROPOSALS 4 (1974), 366-371.

INTEGRATION 5,6,7 I. POLITICAL 2,3	Russett, Bruce M., and W. Curtis Lamb. "Global Patterns of Diplomatic Exchange, 1963-64." JOURNAL OF PEACE RESEARCH, 6, 1 (1969), 37-55.
CRISIS 2 WARFARE 1,2	Russett, Bruce M. NO CLEAR AND PRESENT DANGER: A SKEPTICAL VIEW OF THE U.S. ENTRY INTO WORLD WAR II. New York: Harper and Row, 1972.
WARFARE 3	Russett, Bruce M., Editor. PEACE, WAR, AND NUMBERS. Beverly Hills, Calif.: Sage, 1972.
ARMS 3,6 I. POLITICAL 2,3,b	Russett, Bruce M. WHAT PRICE VIGILANCE? THE BURDENS OF NATIONAL DEFENSE. New Haven, Conn.: Yale University Press, 1970.
I. POLITICAL 2,3 TRANSNATIONAL 3	Russett, Bruce M., Karl Deutsch, Hayward Alker, and Harold D. Lasswell. WORLD HANDBOOK OF POLITICAL AND SOCIAL INDICATORS. New Haven, Conn.: Yale University Press, 1964. See also: Charles David, Taylor, and Michael C. Hudson.
	Russett, Bruce M., see Alker, Hayward R., Jr.
DISARMAMENT 1,2	Saaty, Thomas L. MATHEMATICAL MODELS OF ARMS CONTROL AND DISARMAMENT. New York: Wiley, 1968.
INTEGRATION 4	Saint-Simon, Claude Henri de Rouvroy, comte de; and Augustin Thierry. "The Reorganization of the European Community," translated by Felix Markham, in Blanche Cook, Charles Chatfield, and Sandi Cooper, Editors, FIVE VIEWS ON EUROPEAN PEACE. New York: Garland, 1971 (Orig. pub., 1814).

FUTURES b
SECURITY a

Sakharov, Andrei D. PROGRESS, COEXISTENCE AND INTELLECTUAL FREEDOM. New York: Norton, 1968.

LIBERATION 1,c
WARFARE 1,c

Salert, Barbara. REVOLUTION AND REVOLUTIONARIES: FOUR THEORIES. New York: Elsevier/North-Holland, 1976.

NONVIOLENCE a,b
VIOLENCE 1,2,7

Sampson, Ronald V. THE DISCOVERY OF PEACE. New York: Pantheon Books, 1973.

Sanford, R. Nevitt, see Adorno, Theodore W.

Sapin, Burton, see Snyder, Richard C.

ATTITUDES 1

Sargent, William. BATTLE FOR THE MIND. New York: Doubleday, 1957.

DEVELOPMENT 2,6
I. ECONOMIC 4
TRANSNATIONAL 2,4,6,a

Sauvant, Karl P., and Farid G. Lavipour, Editors. CONTROLLING MULTINATIONAL ENTERPRISES: PROBLEMS, STRATEGIES, COUNTERSTRATEGIES. Boulder, Colo.: Westview, 1976.

DEVELOPMENT 1,b
INTEGRATION 4,6
I. ECONOMIC 1,a
RESOURCES a
TRANSNATIONAL 4,6

Sauvant, Karl P., and Hajo Hasenpflug, Editors. THE NEW INTERNATIONAL ECONOMIC ORDER: CONFRONTATION OR COOPERATION BETWEEN NORTH AND SOUTH? Boulder, Colo.: Westview, 1978.

Sauvant, Karl P., see Mennis, Bernhard.

Schaerf, Carlo, see Carlton, David.

ATTITUDES 1

Schein, Edgar, and Warren Bennis. PERSONAL AND ORGANIZATIONAL CHANGE THROUGH GROUP METHODS. New York: Wiley, 1965.

ARMS 1 I. POLITICAL a VIOLENCE 4	Schelling, Thomas C. ARMS AND INFLUENCE. New Haven, Conn.: Yale University Press, 1966.
DISARMAMENT 1,a I. POLITICAL 1	Schelling, Thomas C. "A Framework for the Evaluation of Arms Proposals," in Martin Pfaff, Editor, FRONTIERS IN SOCIAL THOUGHT: ESSAYS IN HONOR OF KENNETH E. BOULDING. New York: North-Holland, 1976.
CONFLICT 1	Schelling, Thomas C. THE STRATEGY OF CONFLICT. New York: Oxford University Press, 1963.
ARMS 5 MILITARY 4,7	Schevitz, Jeffrey M. THE WEAPONSMAKERS; PERSONAL AND PROFESSIONAL CRISIS DURING THE VIETNAM WAR. Cambridge, Mass.: Schenkman, 1978.
	Schinzel, Luanne, see McGinnis, Kathy.
RESEARCH a,b	Schmid, Herman. "On the Conditions of Applied Social Research"; and "Comments" on the previous article by Lawrence T. Farley. SUMMATION, 3, 2 (Fall 1973), 3-29; 56-59.
RESEARCH b,c,d	Schmid, Herman. "Politics and Peace Research." JOURNAL OF PEACE RESEARCH, 5, 3 (1968), 217-232.
	Schmidt, Fran, see Abrams, Grace (1972, 1973).
	Schmitt, David R., see Marwell, Gerald.
TERRORISM e	Schönborn, Karl L. DEALING WITH VIOLENCE: THE CHALLENGE FACED BY POLICE AND OTHER PEACEKEEPERS. New York: Charles C. Thomas, 1975.

Schou, August, see Eide, Asbjørn.

Schulz, Ann, see Marwah, Ankar.

CONFLICT 2
DEVELOPMENT c
Schurmann, Franz. THE LOGIC OF WORLD POWER: AN INQUIRY INTO THE ORIGINS, CURRENTS, AND CONTRADICTIONS OF WORLD POLITICS. New York: Pantheon, 1974.

FUTURES 1
Schwarz, Stephan, Editor. KNOWLEDGE AND CONCEPTS IN FUTURES STUDIES. Boulder, Colo.: Westview, 1977.

ATTITUDES 5,a
Schwebel, Milton, Editor. BEHAVIORAL SCIENCE AND HUMAN SURVIVAL. Palo Alto, Calif.: Science and Behavior Books, 1965.

DISARMAMENT 2,6,a
SCIENTIFIC AMERICAN. ARMS CONTROL: READINGS FROM SCIENTIFIC AMERICAN. San Francisco: Freeman, 1973.

ARMS 2,4
CONFLICT b
DISARMAMENT 1,a
I. POLITICAL 1
MEDIATION 1,a
VIOLENCE b
WARFARE a
SCIENTIFIC AMERICAN. "War: The Anguish of Renunciation." Section V in SCIENCE, CONFLICT AND SOCIETY: READINGS FROM SCIENTIFIC AMERICAN. San Francisco: Freeman, 1969.

CONFLICT 1
Scott, William. MANAGEMENT OF CONFLICT: APPEAL SYSTEMS IN ORGANIZATIONS. Homewood, Ill.: Irwin, 1965.

Scranton, Margaret E., see Butterworth, Robert Lyle.

Sears, R. R., see Dollard, John.

Segal, David R., see Goldman, Nancy.

CONFLICT 1 MEDIATION a	Senghaas, Dieter. "Conflict Formations in Contemporary International Society." JOURNAL OF PEACE RESEARCH, 10, 3 (1973), 183-184.
RESEARCH a	Senghaas, Dieter, Issue Editor. "Peace Research in the Federal Republic of Germany." JOURNAL OF PEACE RESEARCH 3, 3 (1973).
	Senghaas, Dieter, <u>see</u> Deutsch, Karl W.
CIVILIAN DEF 1 NONVIOLENCE 2	Sharp, Gene. AN ABECEDARY OF NONVIOLENCE ACTION AND CIVILIAN DEFENSE. Cambridge, Mass.: Schenkman, 1972.
CIVILIAN DEF 1,a CONFLICT 4 NONVIOLENCE 1,2,a	Sharp, Gene. EXPLORING NON-VIOLENT ALTERNATIVES. Boston: Porter Sargent, 1970.
NONVIOLENCE 2	Sharp, Gene. GANDHI WIELDS THE WEAPON OF MORAL POWER: THREE CASE HISTORIES. Ahmedabad, India: Navaivan, 1960.
CIVILIAN DEF 1 NONVIOLENCE 1,2	Sharp, Gene. THE POLITICS OF NONVIOLENT ACTION. Boston: Porter Sargent, 1973.
	Sheets, Hal, <u>see</u> Morris, Roger.
	Sherif, Carolyn W., <u>see</u> Sherif, Muzafer.
CONFLICT 2	Sherif, Muzafer, and Carolyn W. Sherif. GROUPS IN HARMONY AND TENSION. New York: Harper, 1953.
CONFLICT 7	Sherif, Muzafer. IN COMMON PREDICAMENT: SOCIAL PSYCHOLOGY OF INTERGROUP CONFLICT AND COOPERATION. Boston: Houghton Mifflin, 1966.

EDUCATION 3 NONVIOLENCE 2	Shivers, Lynn, and Theodore Olson. TRAINING FOR NON-VIOLENT ACTION. Philadelphia: Friends Peace Committee, 1971.
CRISIS 2,4,7 I. POLITICAL 7,a MEDIATION 1,2	Short, Frisco W., Richard G. Head, and Robert C. McFarlane. CRISIS RESOLUTION: PRESIDENTIAL DECISION MAKING IN THE MAYAGUEZ AND KOREAN CONFRONTATIONS. Boulder, Colo.: Westview, 1978.
NONVIOLENCE 2 PROTEST 2,3	Shridharani, Krishnalal. WAR WITHOUT VIOLENCE: THE SOCIOLOGY OF GANDHI'S SATYAGRAHA. New York: Garland, 1971 (Orig. pub., 1939).
CONFLICT 1,b	Shubik, Martin. GAMES FOR SOCIETY, BUSINESS, AND WAR: TOWARD A THEORY OF GAMING. New York: Elsevier, 1975.
CONFLICT 1,b	Shubik, Martin. THE USES AND METHODS OF GAMING. New York: Elsevier, 1975.
CONFLICT 1 NONVIOLENCE 1	Shure, Gerald H., Robert J. Meeker, and Earle A. Hansford. "The Effectiveness of Pacifist Strategies in Bargaining Games." JOURNAL OF CONFLICT RESOLUTION, 9, 1 (March 1965), 106-117.
NONVIOLENCE 1,a,b	Sibley, Mulford Q. THE POLITICAL THEORIES OF MODERN PACIFISM: AN ANALYSIS AND CRITICISM. New York: Garland, 1971 (Orig. pub., 1944).
NONVIOLENCE 2	Sibley, Mulford Q., Editor. THE QUIET BATTLE: WRITINGS ON THE THEORY AND PRACTICE OF NONVIOLENT RESISTANCE. Garden City, N.Y.: Anchor Books, 1963.

CONFLICT 1 INTEGRATION 1,5, 6,7	Simmel, Georg. CONFLICT AND THE WEB OF GROUP AFFILIATIONS. New York: Free Press, 1955.
CONFLICT 4,a DEVELOPMENT 4 MILITARY 4	Simon, Sheldon W., Editor. THE MILITARY AND SECURITY IN THE THIRD WORLD: DOMESTIC AND INTERNATIONAL IMPACTS. Boulder, Colo.: Westview, 1978.
FUTURES b I. ORGANIZATION 1	Simoni, Arnold. BEYOND REPAIR: THE URGENT NEED FOR A NEW WORLD BODY. Donn Mills, Ontario, Canada: Collier-Macmillan, 1972.
	Simons, William E., see George, Alexander L.
RESEARCH a,b	Singer, J. David. "An Assessment of Peace Research." INTERNATIONAL SECURITY, 1, 1 (Summer 1976), 139-154.
I. POLITICAL 1,2, 3,a	Singer, J. David. ON THE SCIENTIFIC STUDY OF POLITICS: AN APPROACH TO FOREIGN POLICY ANALYSIS. New York: General Learning Press, 1972.
I. POLITICAL 1,3	Singer, J. David, Editor. QUANTITATIVE INTERNATIONAL POLITICS: INSIGHTS AND EVIDENCE. New York: Free Press, 1968.
I. POLITICAL 2,3	Singer, J. David, and Melvin Small. THE WAGES OF WAR, 1816-1965: A STATISTICAL HANDBOOK. New York: Wiley, 1972.
VIOLENCE 7	Singer, Jerome L., Editor. THE CONTROL OF AGGRESSION AND VIOLENCE: COGNITIVE AND PHYSIOLOGICAL FACTORS. New York, London: Academic Press, 1971.

DEVELOPMENT c
I. POLITICAL a

Singer, Marshall R. WEAK STATES IN A WORLD OF POWERS: THE DYNAMICS OF INTERNATIONAL RELATIONS. New York: Macmillan, 1972.

Singer, Robert D., see Feshbach, Seymour.

Singh, Yogendra, see Unnithan, T. K. Narayanan.

DEVELOPMENT 4,6
I. ECONOMIC 4
I. POLITICAL 6

Sinha, Radha. FOOD AND POVERTY: THE POLITICAL ECONOMY OF CONFRONTATION. New York: Holmes and Meier, 1976.

CONFLICT 1

Sisson, Roger L., and Russell L. Ackoff. "Toward a Theory of the Dynamics of Conflict." PEACE RESEARCH SOCIETY (INTERNATIONAL) PAPERS, 5 (1966), 187-197.

RESEARCH b

Sjoberg, Gideon. "Project Camelot: Selected Reactions and Personal Reflections," in Gideon Sjoberg, Editor, ETHICS, POLITICS AND SOCIAL RESEARCH. Cambridge, Mass.: Schenkman, 1967.

I. ORGANIZATION 1
TRANSNATIONAL 1

Skjelsbaek, Kjell. "Peace and the Structure of the International Organization Network." JOURNAL OF PEACE RESEARCH, 4 (1972), 315-330.

I. POLITICAL a

Skjelsbaek, Kjell. "Value Incompatibilities in the Global System." JOURNAL OF PEACE RESEARCH, 10, 4 (1973), 341-354.

Skolnick, Paul, see Pilisuk, Marc.

Sloan, Thomas J., see Azar, Edward E.

CONFLICT 1	Small, Albion. GENERAL SOCIOLOGY: AN EXPOSITION OF THE MAIN DEVELOPMENT IN SOCIOLOGICAL THEORY FROM SPENCER TO RATZENHOFER. Chicago: University of Chicago Press, 1925.
	Small, Melvin, see Singer, J. David.
	Smith, Bruce L, see Cohen, Stephen P.
CONFLICT 1 MEDIATION a	Smith, Clagett G., Editor. CONFLICT RESOLUTION: CONTRIBUTIONS OF THE BEHAVIORAL SCIENCES. Notre Dame, Indiana: University of Notre Dame Press, 1971.
MILITARY 6	Smith, Dan, Editor. ALTERNATIVE WORK FOR MILITARY INDUSTRIES; MILITARY SPENDING AND ARMS CUTS: ECONOMIC AND INDUSTRIAL IMPLICATIONS. London: Richardson Institute for Conflict and Peace Research, 1977.
	Smith, Dan, see Elliott, Dave.
CRISIS c	Smith, David S., Editor. FROM WAR TO PEACE: ESSAYS IN PEACEMAKING AND WAR TERMINATION. New York: Columbia University Press, 1974.
	Smith, Ron, see Elliott, Dave.
INTEGRATION 2	Smock, David R., and Kwamena Bentsi-Enchill, Editors. THE SEARCH FOR NATIONAL INTEGRATION IN AFRICA. New York: Free Press, 1976.
I. POLITICAL e	Smoker, Paul. "International Relations Simulations." PEACE RESEARCH REVIEWS, 3, 6 (1970).

	Smoker, Paul, see Newcombe, Alan G.
CONFLICT 7 I. POLITICAL 1 VIOLENCE 5	Snyder, Glenn H., Editor. STUDIES IN INTERNATIONAL CONFLICT. Buffalo: State University of New York at Buffalo, 1968.
I. POLITICAL a	Snyder, Richard C., H. W. Bruck, and Burton Sapin, Editors. FOREIGN POLICY DECISION-MAKING. New York: Free Press, 1962.
	Snyder, Richard C., see Guetzkow, Harold S.; Mack, Raymond; Pruitt, Dean G.; Robinson, James A.
	Sohn, Louis B., see Clark, Grenville (1966, 1973); Price, Charles C.
ATTITUDES 1,b FUTURES 1 NONVIOLENCE 1 WARFARE 1	Somerville, John. THE PEACE REVOLUTION: ETHOS AND SOCIAL PROCESS. Westport, Conn.: Greenwood, 1975.
CONFLICT 5,d VIOLENCE 1	Sorel, Georges. REFLECTIONS ON VIOLENCE. New York: Collier, 1961.
FUTURES b	Sorokin, Pitirim A. "The Conditions and Prospects for a World Without War." AMERICAN JOURNAL OF SOCIOLOGY, 49, 5 (March 1944), 441-449.
VIOLENCE 5,7 WARFARE 5,7	Sorokin, Pitirim A. THE CRISIS OF OUR AGE: THE SOCIAL AND CULTURAL OUTLOOK. New York: E. P. Dutton, 1941.
ATTITUDES 2,a	Sorokin, Pitirim A., and Walter Lunde. POWER AND MORALITY. Boston: Porter Sargent, 1958.

VIOLENCE 7
WARFARE 5,7
Sorokin, Pitirim A. SOCIAL AND CULTURAL DYNAMICS. 4 Volumes. New York: American Book Company, 1937-41. Also: revised and abridged in one volume, Boston: Porter Sargent, 1957.

WARFARE c
Sorokin, Pitirim A. THE SOCIOLOGY OF REVOLUTION. Revised Edition. New York: Howard Fertig, 1972 (Orig. pub., 1925).

NONVIOLENCE 1
Sorokin, Pitirim A. THE WAYS AND POWER OF LOVE: TYPES, FACTORS, AND TECHNIQUES OF MORAL TRANSFORMATION. Boston: Beacon, 1954.

Sourrouille, Juan V., <u>see</u> Mallon, Richard D.

VIOLENCE 4,5,7
Southwood, Ken. "Riot and Revolt: Sociological Theories of Political Violence." PEACE RESEARCH REVIEWS, 1, 3 (1967).

ATTITUDES 1,5
MILITARY 5
WARFARE 1,2,a
Speier, Hans. SOCIAL ORDER AND THE RISKS OF WAR: PAPERS IN POLITICAL SOCIOLOGY. Cambridge, Mass.: MIT Press, 1969) (Orig. pub., 1952).

WARFARE 1
Speier, Hans. "Social Types of War." AMERICAN JOURNAL OF SOCIOLOGY, 46 (January 1941), 445-454.

I. POLITICAL 1
Spiegel, S. L. DOMINANCE AND DIVERSITY: THE INTERNATIONAL HIERARCHY. Boston: Little, Brown, 1972.

I. POLITICAL 1
RESOURCES 4
Sprout, Harold, and Margaret Sprout. TOWARDS A POLITICS OF THE PLANET EARTH. New York: Van Nostrand Reinhold, 1971.

	Sprout, Margaret, see Sprout, Harold.
CONFLICT 1,2	Stagner Ross. THE DIMENSIONS OF HUMAN CONFLICT. Detroit: Wayne State University Press, 1967.
CONFLICT 1,4,5 INTEGRATION 4,5 VIOLENCE 1,4,5,7	Stagner, Ross. "Egocentrism, Ethnocentrism, Altrocentrism--Relations to Individual and Group Violence." INTERNATIONAL JOURNAL OF INTERCULTURAL RELATIONS (1978), 9-30.
I. POLITICAL 7	Stagner, Ross. PSYCHOLOGICAL ASPECTS OF INTERNATIONAL CONFLICT. Monterey, Calif.: Brooks/Cole Division, Wadsworth, 1967.
ATTITUDES 1,d CONFLICT 1,2 FUTURES 1 MEDIATION 1,2	Stanford, Barbara, Editor. PEACEMAKING: A GUIDE TO CONFLICT RESOLUTION FOR INDIVIDUALS, GROUPS, AND NATIONS. New York: Bantam, 1976.
CONFLICT 1 INTEGRATION 1 RESEARCH a	Stein, Arthur A. "Conflict and Cohesion: A Review of the Literature." JOURNAL OF CONFLICT RESOLUTION, 20, 1 (March 1976), 143-172.
INTEGRATION 2 MEDIATION 2	Steiner, Jurg. AMICABLE AGREEMENT VERSUS MAJORITY RULE: CONFLICT RESOLUTION IN SWITZERLAND. Revised Edition. Chapel Hill: University of North Carolina Press, 1974.
CONFLICT 1,5,7 VIOLENCE 1,5,7,a	Steinmetz, Suanne K., and Murray A. Straus, Editors. VIOLENCE IN THE FAMILY. New York: Dodd, Mead, 1974.

ARMS 1,2 I. POLITICAL 1,2 MILITARY 1,2,4,5	Stern, Ellen, Editor. THE LIMITS OF MILITARY INTERVENTION. Inter-University Seminar on Armed Forces and Society. Beverly Hills, Calif.: Sage, 1977.
DEVELOPMENT c DISARMAMENT 6,b I. ECONOMIC 1,2,3 MILITARY 1	Stevenson, Paul. "The Military-Industrial Complex: An examination of the Nature of Corporate Capitalism in America." JOURNAL OF POLITICAL AND MILITARY SOCIOLOGY, 1 (Fall 1973), 247-259.
NONVIOLENCE 1,2,4, 7,a PROTEST 2,4,7	Stiehm, Judith. NONVIOLENT POWER: ACTIVE AND PASSIVE RESISTANCE IN AMERICA. Lexington, Mass.: D. C. Heath, 1972.
ARMS 2,b DISARMAMENT 1,2, 5,6	Stockholm International Peace Research Institute. ARMAMENTS AND DISARMAMENT IN THE NUCLEAR AGE--A HANDBOOK. New York: Humanities Press, 1976.
DISARMAMENT 2	Stockholm International Peace Research Institute. ARMS CONTROL: A SURVEY AND APPRAISAL OF MULTILATERAL AGREEMENTS. London: Taylor and Francis, 1978.
ARMS 4 I. ECONOMIC 4	Stockholm International Peace Research Institute. ARMS TRADE REGISTERS: THE ARMS TRADE WITH THE THIRD WORLD. Stockholm: Almqvist and Wiksell, 1975.
ARMS 2,3,6 DEVELOPMENT a,b,c I. ECONOMIC 3,4	Stockholm International Peace Research Institute. THE ARMS TRADE WITH THE THIRD WORLD. New York: Humanities Press, 1971.

DISARMAMENT 1,2, 3,a	Stockholm International Peace Research Institute. CHEMICAL DISARMAMENTS: SOME PROBLEMS OF VERIFICATION. New York: Humanities Press, 1973.
MILITARY 4	Stockholm International Peace Research Institute. THE MEANING AND MEASUREMENT OF MILITARY EXPENDITURE. Stockholm: Stockholm International Peace Research Institute, 1973.
DISARMAMENT a I. POLITICAL a	Stockholm International Peace Research Institute. THE NEAR-NUCLEAR NATIONS AND THE NON-PROLIFERATION TREATY. New York: Humanities Press, 1972.
DISARMAMENT a	Stockholm International Peace Research Institute. NUCLEAR PROLIFERATION PROBLEMS. Cambridge, Mass.: MIT Press, 1974.
WARFARE a	Stockholm International Peace Research Institute. THE PROBLEM OF CHEMICAL AND BIOLOGICAL WARFARE. 6 Volumes. New York: Humanities Press, 1973.
DEVELOPMENT c MILITARY 4	Stockholm International Peace Research Institute. RESOURCES DEVOTED TO MILITARY RESEARCH AND DEVELOPMENT: AN INTERNATIONAL COMPARISON. New York: Humanities Press, 1972.
DISARMAMENT 1 I. POLITICAL a,f SECURITY e	Stockholm International Peace Research Institute. STRATEGIC DISARMAMENT, VERIFICATION AND NATIONAL SECURITY. London: Taylor and Francis, 1977.

FUTURES 6 RESOURCES a,b TRANSNATIONAL 1	Stockholm International Peace Research Institute. TOWARDS A BETTER USE OF THE OCEANS. New York: Humanities Press, 1969.
CRISIS b I. POLITICAL 7,a WARFARE 2	Stoessinger, John G. WHY NATIONS GO TO WAR. New York: St. Martin's, 1971.
VIOLENCE 4 WARFARE 4	Stohl, Michael. WAR AND DOMESTIC POLITICAL VIOLENCE: THE AMERICAN CAPACITY FOR REPRESSION AND REACTION. Preface by Ted Robert Gurr. Beverly Hills, Calif.: Sage, 1976.
ARMS 2 DISARMAMENT 1,2,4	Stone, Jeremy J. CONTAINING THE ARMS RACE: SOME SPECIFIC PROPOSALS. Cambridge, Mass.: MIT Press, 1966.
VIOLENCE 7,b	Storr, Anthony. HUMAN AGGRESSION. New York: Atheneum, 1968.
ATTITUDES 2,5 VIOLENCE 7,b WARFARE 1,2	Strachey, Alix. THE UNCONSCIOUS MOTIVES OF WAR. New York: International Universities Press, 1957.
	Straus, Murray A., *see* Steinmetz, Suanne K.
	Strong, George W., *see* Laulicht, Jerome; Paul, John.
DEVELOPMENT a,b,d	Sumberg, Theodore A. FOREIGN AID AS MORAL OBLIGATION. Beverly Hills, Calif.: Sage, 1973.
VIOLENCE 5 WARFARE 1,2	Sumner, William Graham. WAR AND OTHER ESSAYS. New Haven, Conn.: Yale University Press, 1911.

INTEGRATION 2,4,a I. ORGANIZATION 2,a TRANSNATIONAL 2, 4,a	Sundelius, Bengt. MANAGING TRANSNATIONALISM IN NORTHERN EUROPE. Boulder, Colo.: Westview, 1978.
ATTITUDES 1 FUTURES b INTEGRATION 1	Suri, Surindar. "Civilization of Peace." INTERDISCIPLINE, 10, 4 (Winter 1973), 53-71.
MEDIATION b MILITARY b	Swift, Richard N. "United Nations Military Training for Peace." INTERNATIONAL ORGANIZATION, 28, 2 (Spring 1974), 267-280.
CONFLICT 1,2,4,5,b	Swingle, Paul G., Editor. THE STRUCTURE OF CONFLICT. New York: Academic Press, 1970.
CONFLICT 7,e INTEGRATION 5,7	Swinth, Robert L. "The Establishment of the Trust Relationship." JOURNAL OF CONFLICT RESOLUTION, 11, 3 (September 1967), 335-344.
	Sylvan, D. A., <u>see</u> Bobrow, Davis B.
ARMS 2,b DISARMAMENT 2,4 I. POLITICAL 1,2	Tampere Peace Research Institute. INTERNATIONAL DETENTE AND DISARMAMENT: CONTRIBUTIONS BY FINNISH AND SOVIET SCHOLARS. Tampere, Finland: Tampere Peace Research, 1977.
DEVELOPMENT 4,6 INTEGRATION 2,b I. ECONOMIC 2,4 I. ORGANIZATION 2,a I. POLITICAL 2,6	Tancer, Shoshana B. ECONOMIC NATIONALISM IN LATIN AMERICA: THE QUEST FOR ECONOMIC INDEPENDENCE. New York: Praeger, 1976.
CONFLICT 2,3 I. POLITICAL 2,3	Tanter, Raymond. "Dimensions of Conflict Behavior Within and Between Nations, 1958-60." JOURNAL OF CONFLICT RESOLUTION, 10, 1 (March 1966), 41-64.

VIOLENCE 7
WARFARE 1,2
Tanter, Raymond. "International War and Domestic Turmoil: Some Contemporary Evidence," in Hugh Davis Graham and Ted Robert Gurr, Editors, VIOLENCE IN AMERICA: HISTORICAL AND COMPARATIVE PERSPECTIVES. National Commission on the Causes and Prevention of Violence. New York: Bantam Books, 1969.

MEDIATION a
Tanter, Raymond. MODELLING AND MANAGING INTERNATIONAL CONFLICT: THE BERLIN CRISIS. Beverly Hills, Calif.: Sage, 1974.

CONFLICT 1,7
Tanter, Raymond, Issue Editor. "Why Fight? Conflict Models for Strategists and Managers." AMERICAN BEHAVIORAL SCIENTIST, 15, 6 (July-August 1972).

VIOLENCE 7
Targ, Harry R. "Children's Developing Orientations to International Politics." JOURNAL OF PEACE RESEARCH, 2 (1970), 79-98.

Targ, Harry R., *see* Beres, Louis René (1975, 1978).

I. POLITICAL 2,3
Taylor, Charles Davis, and Michael C. Hudson. WORLD HANDBOOK OF POLITICAL AND SOCIAL INDICATORS. Second Edition. New Haven, Conn.: Yale University Press, 1972. *See also*: Russett, Bruce M., *et al.*, 1964.

Taylor, Theodore B., *see* Greenwood, Ted; Willrich, Mason.

DISARMAMENT a
Thant, U. BASIC PROBLEMS OF DISARMAMENT: REPORT OF THE SECRETARY GENERAL. New York: United Nations, 1970.

ARMS 2,6	Thayer, George. THE WAR BUSINESS. New York: Simon and Schuster, 1970.
I. POLITICAL d MEDIATION a WARFARE 2,5,b,c	Thee, Marek. NOTES OF A WITNESS: LAOS AND THE SECOND INDO-CHINESE WAR. New York: Random House, 1973.
ATTITUDES 1 CONFLICT 2 NONVIOLENCE b	Thich Nhat Hanh. VIETNAM--LOTUS IN A SEA OF FIRE. New York: Hill and Wang, 1967.
	Thierry, Augustin, see Saint-Simon, Claude Henri de Rouvroy, comte de.
DISARMAMENT 1,2 FUTURES b	Thomas, Norman. THE PREREQUISITES FOR PEACE. New York: Norton, 1959.
CONFLICT 1,5,7	Thompson, James D. "Organizational Management of Conflict." ADMINISTRATIVE SCIENCE QUARTERLY, 5 (March 1961), 485-521.
EDUCATION 1,b,c	Thorpe, Gerald L. A SUGGESTED PROCEDURE FOR TEACHING A TWELVE WEEK UNIT ON PROBLEMS OF PEACE AND WAR IN THE MODERN WORLD. New York: Institute for World Order, 1968.
CONFLICT 4 WARFARE 1,2	Thucydides. THE PELOPONNESIAN WAR. Translated by Rex Warner. Baltimore: Penguin, 1973.
VIOLENCE b	Tiger, Lionel, and Robin Fox. THE IMPERIAL ANIMAL. New York: Dell, 1972.
WARFARE 1,2,c	Timasheff, Nicholas S. WAR AND REVOLUTION. New York: Sheed and Ward, 1965.

FUTURES 1,2	Tinbergen, Jan, Coordinator; Anthony J. Dolman, Editor; Jan Van Ettinger, Director. RESHAPING THE INTERNATIONAL ORDER, A REPORT TO THE CLUB OF ROME. New York: E. P. Dutton, 1976.
DEVELOPMENT 1 FUTURES 6 I. ECONOMIC 1	Tinbergen, Jan. SHAPING THE WORLD ECONOMY: SUGGESTIONS FOR AN INTERNATIONAL ECONOMIC POLICY. New York: Twentieth Century Fund, 1962.
NONVIOLENCE 2,4	Tinker, Jerry. "The Political Power of Non-Violent Resistance: The Gandhian Technique." WESTERN POLITICAL QUARTERLY, 24 (December 1971).
VIOLENCE 1,7,b	Toch, Hans M. VIOLENT MEN: AN INQUIRY INTO THE PSYCHOLOGY OF VIOLENCE. Chicago: Aldine, 1969.
ATTITUDES c	Tolley, Howard, Jr. CHILDREN AND WAR: POLITICAL SOCIALIZATION TO INTERNATIONAL CONFLICT. New York: Teachers College Press, 1973.
FUTURES b INTEGRATION 5,6,7	Tolstoy, Leo. THE LAW OF LOVE AND THE LAW OF VIOLENCE. New York: Holt, Rinehart and Winston, 1970.
NONVIOLENCE 1,2, a,b	Tolstoy, Leo. TOLSTOY'S WRITINGS ON CIVIL DISOBEDIENCE AND NON-VIOLENCE. New York: Bergman, 1967.
ATTITUDES 1,d	Tolstoy, Leo. WAR--PATRIOTISM--PEACE. Edited by Scott Nearing. New York: Garland, 1971 (Orig. pub., 1926).

ATTITUDES 2 NONVIOLENCE 2,b	Tomkinson, Leonard. STUDIES IN THE THEORY AND PRACTICE OF PEACE AND WAR IN CHINESE HISTORY AND LITERATURE. China: Christian Literature Society, 1940.
	Torney, Judith V., see Buergenthal, Thomas.
	Toscano, James V., see Jacob, Philip.
I. LAW 2 I. POLITICAL 2	Toscano, Mario. THE HISTORY OF TREATIES AND INTERNATIONAL POLITICS. A translation of Storia Dei Trattati e Politica Internationale. Baltimore: Johns Hopkins Press, 1966.
WARFARE 1,2	Toynbee, Arnold. WAR AND CIVILIZATION: SELECTIONS FROM A STUDY OF HISTORY. New York: Oxford University Press, 1950.
CONFLICT 1	Tullock, Gordon. THE SOCIAL DILEMMA: THE ECONOMICS OF WAR AND REVOLUTION. Blacksburg, Va.: University Publications, 1974.
DEVELOPMENT b I. POLITICAL 2	Tuveson, Ernest L. REDEEMER NATION: THE IDEA OF AMERICA'S MILLENIAL ROLE. Chicago: University of Chicago Press, 1968.
WARFARE 1,2	Tzu, Sun. THE ART OF WAR. Oxford, England: Clarendon, 1963.
DISARMAMENT 6	Udis, Bernard, Editor. THE ECONOMIC CONSEQUENCES OF REDUCED MILITARY SPENDING. Lexington, Mass.: Lexington Books, 1973.

ARMS 2,6,b MILITARY 1,2,4,6	Udis, Bernard. FROM GUNS TO BUTTER: TECHNOLOGY ORGANIZATIONS AND REDUCED MILITARY SPENDING IN WESTERN EUROPE. Cambridge, Mass.: Ballinger, 1978.
EDUCATION 1	Ulich, Robert. EDUCATION AND THE IDEA OF MANKIND. New York: Harcourt, Brace and World, 1964.
CONFLICT 3 FUTURES 3 RESEARCH e TRANSNATIONAL 3	Union of International Associations/Mankind 2000. YEARBOOK OF WORLD PROBLEMS AND HUMAN POTENTIAL. First Edition. Brussels: Union of International Associations/Mankind 2000, 1976.
DISARMAMENT 1 MEDIATION b MILITARY b	United Nations. BASIC PROBLEMS OF DISARMAMENT: REPORTS OF THE SECRETARY GENERAL. New York: United Nations Publications, 1970.
DEVELOPMENT 2,4,6 I. ECONOMIC 4 I. POLITICAL 6	United Nations. Department of Economic and Social Affairs. IMPLEMENTATION OF THE INTERNATIONAL DEVELOPMENT STRATEGY: PAPERS FOR THE FIRST OVER-ALL REVIEW AND APPRAISAL OF PROGRESS DURING THE SECOND UNITED NATIONS DEVELOPMENT DECADE. Volumes I and II. New York: United Nations, 1973.
DEVELOPMENT 4,6 I. ECONOMIC 4 I. POLITICAL 6 TRANSNATIONAL 6	United Nations. Department of Economic and Social Affairs. MULTINATIONAL CORPORATIONS IN WORLD DEVELOPMENT. New York: Praeger, 1974.

ARMS 2,3,4,5,6
DEVELOPMENT 2
DISARMAMENT 6
I. ECONOMIC 2,5,a
RESOURCES 6

United Nations. Department of Political and Security Council Affairs. United Nations Centre for Disarmament. ECONOMIC AND SOCIAL CONSEQUENCES OF THE ARMS RACE AND OF MILITARY EXPENDITURES. New York: United Nations, 1978.

ATTITUDES 6
SECURITY a,f

United Nations Educational, Scientific and Cultural Organization. BIRTHRIGHT OF MAN, A SELECTION OF TEXTS PREPARED UNDER THE DIRECTION OF JEANNE HERSCH. Paris: United Nations Educational, Scientific and Cultural Organization, 1969.

CONFLICT 1,5,a
I. POLITICAL a
MEDIATION 1,2,a
VIOLENCE 1

United Nations Institute for Training and Research. PEACEFUL SETTLEMENT OF DISPUTES. New York: United Nations Institute for Training and Research, 1970.

I. POLITICAL 7
MEDIATION a

United Nations Institute for Training and Research. SOCIAL PSYCHOLOGICAL TECHNIQUES AND THE PEACEFUL SETTLEMENT OF INTERNATIONAL DISPUTES. New York: United Nations Institute for Training and Research, 1970.

United Nations. For works about the United Nations, <u>see</u> Alger, Chadwick F. (1972, 1968); Falk, Richard A., and Saul H. Mendlovitz; Higgins, Rosalyn; Pechota, Vratislav; Swift, Richard N.; Thant, U.

DISARMAMENT 6
RESEARCH a

United States Arms Control and Disarmament Agency. THE ECONOMIC IMPACT OF REDUCTIONS IN DEFENSE SPENDING. Washington, D.C.: U.S. Arms Control and Disarmament Agency, 1972.

DISARMAMENT 6	United States Arms Control and Disarmament Agency. ECONOMIC IMPACTS OF DISARMAMENT. Prepared by panel of experts under chairmanship of Emile Benoit. Washington, D.C.: U.S. Government Printing Office, January 1962.
PROTEST 3	United States Congress. Senate Judiciary Committee. FEDERAL HANDLING OF DEMONSTRATIONS. Hearings before Subcommittee on Administrative Practice and Procedure, 91st Congress, 2nd Session, Pursuant to S. Res. 333, Part I. Washington, D.C.: U.S. Government Printing Office, 1970.
NONVIOLENCE 1,7	Unnithan, T. K. Narayanan, and Yogendra Singh. SOCIOLOGY OF NON-VIOLENCE AND PEACE: SOME BEHAVIOURAL AND ATTITUDINAL DIMENSIONS. New Delhi: Research for Cultural Studies, India International Centre, 1969.
	Uphoff, Norman, <u>see</u> Littauer, Rapheal.
DEVELOPMENT a,b,c I. ECONOMIC 4,a I. POLITICAL 6,d	Uri, Pierre. DEVELOPMENT WITHOUT DEPENDENCE. Foreword by William P. Bundy. New York: Praeger, for the Atlantic Institute for International Affairs, 1976.
WARFARE 1,2	Urlanis, B. WARS AND POPULATION. Translated by L. Leupert. Moscow: Progress Publishers, 1971.
MILITARY 2	Vagts, Alfred. A HISTORY OF MILITARISM. Revised Edition. New York: Meridian Books, 1959.

DEVELOPMENT 4,6 I. ECONOMIC 4 I. POLITICAL 6 TRANSNATIONAL 6	Vaitsos, Constantine V. INTER-COUNTRY INCOME DISTRIBUTION AND TRANSNATIONAL ENTERPRISES. New York: Oxford University Press, 1974.
MILITARY 2,5	Van Doorn, Jacques. THE SOLDIER AND SOCIAL CHANGE: COMPARATIVE STUDIES IN THE HISTORY AND SOCIOLOGY OF THE MILITARY. Beverly Hills, Calif.: Sage, 1975.
	Van Doorn, Jacques, <u>see</u> Harries-Jenkins, Gwyn.
	Van Ettinger, Jan, <u>see</u> Tinbergen, Jan.
	Van Krieken, Peter J., <u>see</u> Akkerman, Robert J.
RESOURCES a	Van Raay, Hans G. T., and Ariel E. Lugo, Editors. MAN AND ENVIRONMENT LTD.: NATURAL IMBALANCES AND SOCIAL JUSTICE. Rotterdam: Rotterdam University Press, for the Institute of Social Sciences, The Hague, 1974. Distributed by Academic Book Services, The Netherlands.
RESEARCH a	Vayda, Andrew P., and Anthony Leeds. "Anthropology and the Study of War." ANTHROPOLOGICA, 3, 2 (1961).
I. POLITICAL 5 RESOURCES a WARFARE 2,5	Vayda, Andrew P. WAR IN ECOLOGICAL PERSPECTIVE: PERSISTENCE, CHANGE, AND ADAPTIVE PROCESSES IN THREE OCEANIAN SOCIETIES. New York: Plenum, 1976.
	Vayrynen, Raimo, <u>see</u> Boulding, Elise.

INTEGRATION 4	Veblen, Thorstein. AN INQUIRY INTO THE NATURE OF PEACE AND THE TERMS OF ITS PERPETUATION. Clifton, N.J.: A. M. Kelley, 1964 (Orig. pub., 1917).
DEVELOPMENT 1,6,b FUTURES 1 I. ECONOMIC 1 I. LAW 1	Verwey, Wil. ECONOMIC DEVELOPMENT, PEACE, AND INTERNATIONAL LAW. New York: Humanities Press, 1972.
I. POLITICAL 2	Vigor, P..H. THE SOVIET VIEW OF WAR, PEACE AND NEUTRALITY. London: Routledge and Kegan Paul, 1975.
I. POLITICAL 1	Vincent, R. J. NONINTERVENTION AND INTERNATIONAL ORDER. Princeton, N.J.: Princeton University Press, 1976.
I. POLITICAL 2,3	Vital, David. THE SURVIVAL OF SMALL STATES: STUDIES IN SMALL POWER/GREAT POWER CONFLICT. London: Oxford University Press, 1971.
	Volgyes, Ivan, <u>see</u> Herspring, Dale R.
EDUCATION 1 FUTURES 1,b LIBERATION 1,b	Wagar, W. Warren. BUILDING THE CITY OF MAN: OUTLINES OF A WORLD CIVILIZATION. New York: Grossman, 1971.
MEDIATION 2,b MILITARY 2,b	Wainhouse, David W., <u>et.al</u>. INTERNATIONAL PEACE OBSERVATION: A HISTORY AND FORECAST. Baltimore: Johns Hopkins Press, 1966.
MEDIATION b MILITARY b	Wainhouse, David W. INTERNATIONAL PEACEKEEPING AT THE CROSSROADS. Baltimore: Johns Hopkins Press, 1973.

DEVELOPMENT 1,2, b,c I. POLITICAL 1,2,d	Walbek, Norman V., and Sidney Weintraub, Editors. CONFLICT, ORDER, AND PEACE IN THE AMERICAS. PART I: DIALOGUES ON THE ISSUES. Austin: Lyndon B. Johnson School of Public Affairs, University of Texas, 1978.
ATTITUDES 4 INTEGRATION 4 TRANSNATIONAL 4,6	Walbek, Norman V. "Global Public Political Culture." PEACE RESEARCH REVIEWS, 5, 2 (November 1973).
MEDIATION b MILITARY b	Walker, Charles C. PEACEKEEPING: 1969. Philadelphia: Friends Peace Committee, 1969.
	Walker, Charles, see Cooper, William.
I. POLITICAL a WARFARE a	Wallace, Michael D. "Power, Status and International War." JOURNAL OF PEACE RESEARCH, 1 (1971), 23-36.
INTEGRATION 5,6,7 VIOLENCE 5	Wallace, Michael D. WAR AND RANK AMONG NATIONS. Toronto: Lexington Books, 1973.
	Wallace, Michael D., see Hofstadter, Richard; Newcombe, Alan G.
CRISIS b I. POLITICAL 1,2,3	Wallensteen, Peter. STRUCTURE AND WAR: ON INTERNATIONAL RELATIONS 1920-1968. Stockholm: Raben and Sjögren, 1973.
MILITARY 5 WARFARE 5	Waller, Willard W. ON THE FAMILY, EDUCATION, AND WAR: SELECTED WRITINGS. Edited by William F. Goode, Frank F. Furstenburg, Jr., and Larry R. Mitchell. Chicago: University of Chicago Press, 1970.

FUTURES c TERRORISM 1,d,e VIOLENCE 7	Walter, E. V. TERROR AND RESISTANCE--A STUDY OF POLITICAL VIOLENCE. New York: Oxford University Press, 1969.
DEVELOPMENT 4,6 RESOURCES 4,6,c TRANSNATIONAL 6	Walter, Ingo, Editor. STUDIES IN INTERNATIONAL ENVIRONMENTAL ECONOMICS. New York: Wiley-Interscience, 1976.
	Walters, Robert S., see Blake, David H.
WARFARE 1	Waltz, Kenneth N. MAN, THE STATE AND WAR: A THEORETICAL ANALYSIS. New York: Columbia University Press, for the Institute of War and Peace Studies, 1959.
I. POLITICAL 2,a PROTEST 2	Wank, Soloman, Editor. DOVES AND DIPLOMATS: FOREIGN OFFICES AND PEACE MOVEMENTS IN EUROPE AND AMERICA IN THE 20TH CENTURY. Westport, Conn.: Greenwood, 1978.
CONFLICT 1	Warren, Roland. "The Conflict Intersystem and the Change Agent." JOURNAL OF CONFLICT RESOLUTION, 8, 3 (1964), 231-241.
I. POLITICAL 1 TRANSNATIONAL 5	Washburn, A. Michael, and Thomas G. Weiss. "Shaking Hands With the Invisible Hand--Transnational Strategies for Global Social Change: Questions and Issues." BULLETIN OF PEACE PROPOSALS, 6 (1975), 180-190.
	Washburn, A. Michael, see Beitz, Charles R.; Wehr, Paul (1973, 1976).
DISARMAMENT 1 MEDICATION b MILITARY b	Waskow, Arthur I. KEEPING THE WORLD DIS-ARMED. Santa Barbara, Calif.: Center for the Study of Democratic Institutions, 1965.

ARMS a DISARMAMENT 1,a I. POLITICAL a WARFARE a	Waskow, Arthur I. THE LIMITS OF DEFENSE. New York: Doubleday, 1962.
PROTEST 2	Waskow, Arthur I. RUNNING RIOT. New York: Herder and Herder, 1970.
ATTITUDES 1 WARFARE 1,2	Wasserstrom, Richard A., Editor. WAR AND MORALITY. Belmont, Calif.: Wadsworth, 1970.
I. POLITICAL 3	Waters, Judy, Scott Peters, and Hanna Newcombe. MILESTONE EVENTS. Oakville, Ontario: Canadian Peace Research Institute, 1975.
DISARMAMENT 2	Watson, Lorna. "History of Disarmament Negotiations." PEACE RESEARCH REVIEWS, 1, 2 (April 1967).
VIOLENCE 7 WARFARE 2	Watson, Peter. WAR ON THE MIND: THE MILITARY USES AND ABUSES OF PSYCHOLOGY. New York: Basic Books, 1978.
CONFLICT 1,2,5 EDUCATION a MEDIATION 1,2 PROTEST 2 RESOURCES 4,6	Wehr, Paul. CONFLICT REGULATION. Boulder, Colo.: Westview, 1978.
EDUCATION 1,b,c	Wehr, Paul, and A. Michael Washburn. "Developing Quality Peace Studies Programs." PEACE AND CHANGE, 1, 3 (1973), 4-16.
CONFLICT 2 NONVIOLENCE 2 PROTEST 2	Wehr, Paul. "Nonviolence and Differentiation in the Equal Rights Movement." SOCIOLOGICAL INQUIRY, 38, 1 (Winter 1968), 65-76.
CIVILIAN DEF 2 NONVIOLENCE 2	Wehr, Paul. "Nonviolent Resistance to Occupation: Norway and Czechoslovakia." JOURNAL OF SOCIAL ISSUES, 1974.

EDUCATION b,c
RESEARCH a

Wehr, Paul, and A. Michael Washburn. PEACE AND WORLD ORDER SYSTEMS: TEACHING AND RESEARCH. Beverly Hills, Calif.: Sage, 1976.

ARMS 6
DISARMAMENT 6

Weidenbaum, Murray L. THE ECONOMICS OF PEACETIME DEFENSE. New York: Praeger, 1974.

FUTURES 1
I. POLITICAL 1

Weidenbaum, Murray L. "A New Arms Age," in Martin Pfaff, Editor, FRONTIERS IN SOCIAL THOUGHT: ESSAYS IN HONOR OF KENNETH E. BOULDING. New York: North-Holland, 1976.

DISARMAMENT 6

Weidenbaum, Murray L. "The Transferability of Defense Industry Resources to Civilian Use," in Roger E. Bolton, Editor, DEFENSE AND DISARMAMENT: THE ECONOMICS OF TRANSITION. Englewood Cliffs, N.J.: Prentice-Hall, 1966.

Weiler, Lawrence D., see Barton, John H.; Platt, Alan.

NONVIOLENCE a,b
PROTEST b,c

Weinberg, Arthur, and Lita Weinberg, Editors. INSTEAD OF VIOLENCE: WRITINGS BY THE GREAT ADVOCATES OF PEACE AND NONVIOLENCE THROUGHOUT HISTORY. Boston: Beacon, 1963.

Weinberg, Lita, see Weinberg, Arthur.

Weintraub, Sidney, see Walbek, Norman V.

Weisband, Edward, see Franck, Thomas M.

Weisner, Jerome B., see Dahl, Norman C.

I. ORGANIZATION 2
RESOURCES d

Weiss, Thomas G., and Robert S. Jordan. THE WORLD FOOD CONFERENCE AND GLOBAL PROBLEM SOLVING. New York: Praeger, in cooperation with the United Nations Institute for Training and Research, 1977.

Weiss, Thomas G., see Washburn, A. Michael.

MILITARY 1,2

Welch, Claude E., Jr., Editor. CIVILIAN CONTROL OF THE MILITARY: THEORY AND CASES FROM DEVELOPING COUNTRIES. Albany: State University of New York Press, 1976.

Wenglinsky, Martin, see Etzioni, Amitai.

Werner, Herman, see Preston, Richard A.

Wert, James, see Newcombe, Alan G.

ARMS b
WARFARE a,b

Westing, Arthur H. WEAPONS OF MASS DESTRUCTION AND THE ENVIRONMENT. London: Taylor and Francis, 1977.

Weston, Burns H., see Reisman, W. Michael.

ATTITUDES 2

White, Ralph K. "Misperception and the Vietnam War." JOURNAL OF SOCIAL ISSUES, 22, 3 (July 1966).

ATTITUDES 2

White, Ralph K. "Misperception in the Arab-Conflict." JOURNAL OF SOCIAL ISSUES, 33, 1 (1977), 190-221.

ATTITUDES 2

White, Ralph K. NOBODY WANTED WAR: MISPERCEPTION IN VIETNAM AND OTHER WARS. New York: Doubleday, 1970.

	White, Ralph K., see Eckhardt, William.
ATTITUDES 2,5,6 NONVIOLENCE 7,b,c	Whitney, Kendall A. PACIFISM IN JAPANESE POLITICS AND SOCIETY. Boulder, Colo.: Westview, 1978.
ATTITUDES b FUTURES b	WHOLE EARTH PAPERS. Special Issue: "Christian Voices on World Order," 1, 9 (1978).
FUTURES b	WHOLE EARTH PAPERS. Special Issue: "Indian Voices on World Order," 1, 5 (Winter 1978).
VIOLENCE 7,b WARFARE 1	"Why is Man Aggressive? A Synthetic Round Table." IMPACT OF SCIENCE ON SOCIETY, 18, 2 (April-June 1968), 85-95.
	Whyte, William Foote, see Hall, Edward T.
	Wiener, Anthony J., see Kahn, Herman.
DISARMAMENT 1,2 EDUCATION 1 I. ORGANIZATION 2 RESEARCH a	Wihtol, Robert, Editor. RESEARCH, EDUCATION AND INFORMATION ON DISARMAMENT. Helsinki: Ministry of Education, 1978.
CONFLICT 1 VIOLENCE 5	Wilkenfeld, Jonathan, Editor. CONFLICT BEHAVIOR AND LINKAGE POLITICS. New York: David McKay, 1973.
TRANSNATIONAL 2,6	Wilkins, Mira. THE MATURING OF MULTINATIONAL ENTERPRISE: AMERICAN BUSINESS ABROAD FROM 1914 TO 1970. Cambridge, Mass.: Harvard University Press, 1974.
TERRORISM 4	Wilkinson, Paul. POLITICAL TERRORISM. New York: Wiley, 1974.

DEVELOPMENT 1 RESOURCES 1,a	Wilkinson, Richard G. POVERTY AND PROGRESS: AN ECOLOGICAL PERSPECTIVE ON ECONOMIC DEVELOPMENT. Introduction by Kenneth E. Boulding. New York: Praeger, 1973.
I. ECONOMIC 4 I. ORGANIZATION 1 I. POLITICAL 6 RESOURCES 4,6,a,b	Willrich, Mason. ENERGY AND WORLD POLITICS. New York: Free Press, for the American Society of International Law, 1975.
ARMS 4 TERRORISM d,e	Willrich, Mason, and Theodore B. Taylor. NUCLEAR THEFT: RISKS AND SAFEGUARDS. Cambridge, Mass.: Ballinger, 1974.
DISARMAMENT 2,a	Willrich, Mason, and J. B. Rhinelander. SALT: THE MOSCOW AGREEMENTS AND BEYOND. New York: Free Press, 1974.
	Wise, Sydney, see Preston, Richard A.
	Woito, Robert, see Pickus, Robert.
	Wolf, Charles, see Leites, Nathan.
WARFARE 2,b,c	Wolf, Eric R. PEASANT WARS OF THE TWENTIETH CENTURY. New York: Harper and Row, 1969.
I. ECONOMIC 1,2	Wolf, Thomas A. U.S. EAST-WEST TRADE POLICY: ECONOMIC WARFARE VERSUS ECONOMIC WELFARE. Lexington, Mass.: Lexington Books, 1973.
ATTITUDES 4 CONFLICT 4,7,a,c RESEARCH b	Woodward, Beverly. "Peace Studies and the Feminist Challenge." PEACE AND CHANGE: A JOURNAL OF PEACE RESEARCH, 3, 4 (Spring 1976), 3-12.

CIVILIAN DEF 1,b CONFLICT 7 DISARMAMENT 3,4, 6,a INTEGRATION 5	Wright, Quincy, William M. Evan, and Morton Deutsch, Editors. PREVENTING WORLD WAR III: SOME PROPOSALS. New York: Simon and Schuster, 1962.
I. LAW 1,2,a,d WARFARE 1	Wright, Quincy. THE ROLE OF INTERNATIONAL LAW IN THE ELIMINATION OF WAR. New York: Oceana, 1961.
I. POLITICAL 1	Wright, Quincy. THE STUDY OF INTERNATIONAL RELATIONS. New York: Appleton-Century-Crofts, 1955.
ARMS 1,2 INTEGRATION 1,2 I. LAW 1,2 I. ORGANIZATION 2 I. POLITICAL 1,2, a,b,c RESEARCH a,b WARFARE 1,2	Wright, Quincy. A STUDY OF WAR. Second Edition, with commentary on war since 1942. Chicago: University of Chicago Press, 1965 (Orig. pub., 1942).
INTEGRATION 1,2,5 I. ORGANIZATION 1	Wright, Quincy, Editor. THE WORLD COMMUNITY. Chicago: University of Chicago Press, 1948.
EDUCATION 1,2	Wulf, Christoph, Editor. HANDBOOK ON PEACE EDUCATION. Frankfurt: Education Committee of the International Peace Research Association, 1974.
FUTURES b	Wynner, Edith, and Georgia Lloyd. SEARCHLIGHT ON PEACE PLANS. New York: Dutton, 1946.
MILITARY 2,4	Yarmolinsky, Adam. THE MILITARY ESTABLISHMENT. New York: Harper and Row, 1971.
VIOLENCE 5 WARFARE c	Yarmolinsky, Avrahm. ROAD TO REVOLUTION. New York: Collier Books, 1968.

MEDIATION 2,a NONVIOLENCE 2	Yarrow, C. H. Mike. QUAKER EXPERIENCES IN INTERNATIONAL CONCILIATION. New Haven, Conn.: Yale University Press, 1978.
ARMS 1,2,4 DISARMAMENT a I. POLITICAL a,f	Yergin, Daniel. SHATTERED PEACE: THE ORIGINS OF THE COLD WAR AND THE NATIONAL SECURITY STATE. Boston: Houghton Mifflin, 1977.
ARMS 2,b DISARMAMENT a I. POLITICAL a	York, Herbert F. THE ADVISORS: OPPENHEIMER AND TELLER AND THE SUPERBOMB. San Francisco: Freeman, 1976.
DISARMAMENT a	York, Herbert F. RACE TO OBLIVION: A PARTICIPANT'S VIEW OF THE ARMS RACE. New York: Harper and Row, 1970.
DEVELOPMENT c INTEGRATION 4	Yost, Charles. THE INSECURITY OF NATIONS. New York: Praeger, 1968.
	Young, Christopher, see Eckhardt, William.
CONFLICT 1 INTEGRATION 1 MEDIATION 1	Young, Oran R., Editor. BARGAINING: FORMAL THEORIES OF NEGOTIATION. Chicago: University of Illinois Press, 1975.
CRISIS a I. POLITICAL 1 MEDIATION 1	Young, Oran R. THE INTER-MEDIARIES: THIRD PARTIES IN INTERNATIONAL CRISES. Princeton, N.J.: Princeton University Press, 1967.
	Zacher, Joseph, see Bard, Morton.
	Zaninovich, M. George, see North, Robert C.
WARFARE a,b	Zawodny, J. K. "Unconventional Warfare." AMERICAN SCHOLAR, 31, 3 (Summer 1962), 384-394.

DEVELOPMENT b

Zeylstra, William Gustaaf. AID OR DEVELOPMENT: THE RELEVANCE OF DEVELOPMENT AID TO PROBLEMS OF DEVELOPING COUNTRIES. Leyden, The Netherlands: A. W. Sijthoff, 1975. Distributed by Academic Book Services, The Netherlands.

RESEARCH a,b

Zinnes, Dina A. CONTEMPORARY RESEARCH IN INTERNATIONAL RELATIONS: A PERSPECTIVE AND A CRITICAL APPRAISAL. New York: Free Press, 1976.

Zinnes, Dina A., <u>see</u> North, Robert C.

Collections, Annuals, and Series

Commission to Study the Organization of Peace. BUILDING PEACE: REPORTS OF THE COMMISSION TO STUDY THE ORGANIZATION OF PEACE, 1939-1972. 2 Volumes. Metuchen, N.J.: Scarecrow Press, 1973.

Cook, Blanche Wiesen, Charles Chatfield, and Sandi Cooper, Editors. GARLAND LIBRARY OF WAR AND PEACE. New York: Garland. A collection of 360 reprinted titles.

Cordier, Andrew W., Wilder Foote, and Max Harrelson, Editors. PUBLIC PAPERS OF THE SECRETARIES-GENERAL OF THE UNITED NATIONS. New York: Columbia University Press, 1974--.

Davis, Vincent, Editor. SAGE PROFESSIONAL PAPERS IN INTERNATIONAL STUDIES. Beverly Hills, California: Sage, 1970--.

Falk, Richard A., and Cyril E. Black, Editors. THE FUTURE OF THE INTERNATIONAL LEGAL ORDER. 4 Volumes. Princeton, N.J.: Princeton University Press, 1969--.

Falk, Richard A., and Saul H. Mendlovitz, Editors. REGIONAL POLITICS AND WORLD ORDER. San Francisco: Freeman, 1973. A continuation of THE STRATEGY OF WORLD ORDER series.

Falk, Richard A., and Saul H. Mendlovitz, Editors. THE STRATEGY OF WORLD ORDER. 4 Volumes. New York: Institute for World Order, 1966.

Falk, Richard A., Editor. THE VIETNAM WAR AND INTERNATIONAL LAW. Princeton, N.J.: Princeton University Press, 1967.

Fogelson, Robert, and Richard Rubenstein. MASS VIOLENCE IN AMERICA. 43 Volumes. New York: Arno, 1970.

Galtung, Johan. ESSAYS IN PEACE RESEARCH. Copenhagen: Christian Ejlers, 1975--.

International Institute for Strategic Studies, London. THE MILITARY BALANCE. Annually, 1959-60--. Boulder, Colo.: Westview.

International Peace Research Association, IPRA STUDIES IN PEACE RESEARCH. 6 Volumes. Volumes 1,2,4: Assen, The Netherlands: Royal Van Gorcum, 1966, 1968, 1970. Volumes 3,5,6: Oslo: International Peace Research Association, 1969, 1973, 1974.

Isard, Walter, Editor. MAJOR PEACE TREATIES OF MODERN HISTORY, 1648-1966. 4 Volumes. Introduction by Arnold Toynbee. New York: Chelsea House/McGraw-Hill, 1967.

Isard, Walter, and Juliet Wolpert, Editors. PEACE SCIENCE SOCIETY (INTERNATIONAL) PAPERS. Annually, 1964--. Philadelphia: Department of Regional Science, University of Pennsylvania. Former title: PEACE RESEARCH SOCIETY (INTERNATIONAL) PAPERS.

Kriesberg, Louis, Editor. RESEARCH IN SOCIAL MOVEMENTS, CONFLICT, AND CHANGE. Annually, 1978--. Greenwich, Conn.: JAI Press.

London Institute of World Affairs. THE YEARBOOK OF WORLD AFFAIRS. Annually, 1975--. London: Stevens and Sons.

Melman, Seymour, Editor. CONVERSION OF INDUSTRY FROM A MILITARY TO CIVILIAN ECONOMY. New York: Praeger, 1970--.

Moskos, Charles C., Jr., and Sam C. Sarkesian, Editors. SAGE RESEARCH PROGRESS SERIES ON WAR, REVOLUTION, AND PEACEKEEPING. 6 Volumes. Beverly Hills, Calif.: Sage, 1971--.

PAPERS. The Defense Department History of United States Decision-making on Vietnam. 5 Volumes. Boston: Beacon, 1971.

PEACE PLANS. Irregularly, 1964--. J. M. Zube, Editor. Wilshire Street, Berrima, New South Wales 2577, Australia.

Rohn, Peter H. WORLD TREATY INDEX: TREATY PROFILES. 5 Volumes. Santa Barbara, Calif.: American Bibliographical Center-Clio, 1974.

Schindler, Dietrich, and Jiri Toman. THE LAWS OF ARMED CONFLICTS: A COLLECTION OF CONVENTIONS, RESOLUTIONS AND OTHER DOCUMENTS. Leiden, The Netherlands: Sijthoff, 1973.

Sivard, Ruth Leger. WORLD MILITARY AND SOCIAL EXPENDITURES. Annually. Leesburg, Va.: WMSE Publications.

Stockholm International Peace Research Institute. WORLD ARMAMENTS AND DISARMAMENT: SIPRI YEARBOOK. Annually, 1969-- (except 1971). Cambridge, Mass.: MIT Press. Title varies.

Union of International Associations. YEARBOOK OF INTERNATIONAL ORGANIZATIONS. Annually. Brussels: Union of International Associations.

Union of International Associations. YEARBOOK OF WORLD PROBLEMS AND HUMAN POTENTIAL. Annually, 1976--. Brussels: Union of International Associations.

United States. Arms Control and Disarmament Agency. DOCUMENTS ON DISARMAMENT. Annually, 1960--. Washington, D.C.: U.S. Government Printing Office.

United States. National Commission on the Causes and Prevention of Violence. REPORTS, and FINAL REPORT. Washington, D.C.: U.S. Government Printing Office, 1969.

Walker, Charles, Editor. MONOGRAPH SERIES ON NONVIOLENT ACTION. Haverford, Pa.: Center for Nonviolent Conflict Resolution. Series available from Editor. Haverford College, Haverford, Pennsylvania 19141.

War Resisters' International. ARCHIVES OF WAR RESISTERS' INTERNATIONAL, 1921-1974. Sussex, England: Harvester Press, 1977. Microfiche.

WHOLE EARTH PAPERS. 1978--. Global Education Associates, 552 Park Avenue, East Orange, New Jersey 07017.

Periodicals

ALTERNATIVES: A JOURNAL FOR WORLD POLICY. Quarterly, 1975--. Rajni Kothari, General Editor. North-Holland Publishing Company, 52 Vanderbilt Avenue, New York, New York 10017.

AMNESTY ACTION. Monthly, 1967--. Lorrin Rosenbaum, Editor. Amnesty International of the U.S.A., 200 West 72nd Street, Suite 64, New York, New York 10023.

AMNESTY INTERNATIONAL NEWSLETTER. Monthly, 1963--. Amnesty International, 53 Theobold's Road, London WC1X 8SP, England.

ANOTHER MOTHER FOR PEACE. Quarterly, 1967--. Barbara Avedon and Dorothy Jones, Editors. 407 North Maple, Beverly Hills, California 90210.

ARMED FORCES AND SOCIETY: AN INTERDISCIPLINARY JOURNAL ON MILITARY INSTITUTIONS, CIVIL-MILITARY RELATIONS, ARMS CONTROL AND PEACEKEEPING, AND CONFLICT MANAGEMENT. Quarterly, 1974--. Inter-University Seminar on Armed Forces and Society, Social Science Building, University of Chicago, Chicago, Illinois 60637.

A.W.I.N. NEWSLETTER. Monthly, 1967--. Atlanta Workshop in Nonviolence, Box 7477, Atlanta, Georgia 30309.

BULLETIN OF PEACE PROPOSALS. Quarterly, 1970--. Publication of the International Peace Research Institute, Oslo. U.S. address: Universitets-forlaget, P. O. Box 142, Boston, Massachusetts 02113.

BULLETIN OF THE ATOMIC SCIENTISTS. Monthly (September-June), 1945--. Samuel H. Day, Jr., Editor. Education Foundation for Nuclear Science, 1020-24 East 58 Street, Chicago, Illinois 60637. Some issues have title: SCIENCE AND PUBLIC AFFAIRS.

C.C.C.O. NEWS NOTES. 5 issues per year, 1949--. Robert Seeley, Editor. C.C.C.O., An Agency for Military and Draft Counseling, 2016 Walnut Street, Philadelphia, Pennsylvania 19103.

Center for Teaching About Peace and War. NEWSLETTER. Quarterly, 1965--. Wayne State University, 5229 Cass Avenue, Room 101, Detroit, Michigan 48202.

COMBAT NON VIOLENT. Weekly, 1971--. Communaute Non Violence, 50 rue d'Illiers, 4500 Orleans, France.

CONFLICT: AN INTERNATIONAL JOURNAL. Quarterly, 1978--. Publication of the National Strategy Information Center, New York. Crane, Russak and Company, 347 Madison Avenue, New York, New York 10017.

CONFLICT STUDIES. Monthly, 1969--. Brian Crozier, Editor. Institute for the Study of Conflict, 17 Northumberland Avenue, London WC2N 5BJ, England.

COOPERATION AND CONFLICT: NORDIC STUDIES IN INTERNATIONAL POLITICS. Quarterly, 1965--. U.S. address: Universitetsforlaget, P. O. Box 142, Boston, Massachusetts 02113.

CURRENT RESEARCH ON PEACE AND VIOLENCE. Quarterly, 1971--. Raimo Väyrynen, Editor. Tampere Peace Research Institute, Tammelanpuistokatu 58 BV 33 100, Tampere 10, Finland. Former title: INSTANT RESEARCH ON PEACE AND VIOLENCE.

DEFENSE INDUSTRY BULLETIN. Office of Assistant Secretary of Defense (Public Affairs), The Pentagon, Washington, D.C. 20301.

FELLOWSHIP. Monthly, 1935--. Fellowship of Reconciliation, Box 271, Nyack, New York 10960.

GANDHI MARG: JOURNAL OF THE GANDHI PEACE FOUNDATION. Quarterly, 1957--. G. Ramachandran and T. K. Mahadevan, Editors. T. K. Mahadevan, 221-223 Deen Dayal Upadhyaya Marg, New Delhi 110-001, India.

GUERRES ET PAIX/WARS AND PEACE. Quarterly, 1966--. Gaston Bouthoul and Louise Weiss, Editors. French Institute of Polemology, 15 Avenue du President Wilson, 75 Paris (6e), France. Text in French; summaries in English, German, and Spanish.

HERALD OF PEACE AND INTERNATIONAL ARBITRATION. Irregularly, 1819--. International Peace Society, 195-7 Walworth Road, London S.W. 1, England.

HUMAN RIGHTS BULLETIN. Semi-annually, 1969--. Division of Human Rights, United Nations, Palais des Nations, 1211 Geneva 10, Switzerland. Distributed also by the United Nations Headquarters, New York, New York 10017. In English, French, Russian, and Spanish.

IMPACT OF SCIENCE ON SOCIETY. Quarterly, 1950--. United Nations Educational, Scientific, and Cultural Organization, Place de Fontenoy, 75 Paris (7e), France.

INFORMATION FROM THE PEACE MOVEMENT OF THE GERMAN DEMOCRATIC REPUBLIC. Monthly, 1960--. Peace Council of the German Democratic Republic, Clara-Zetkin-Str. 103, 108 Berlin, East Germany.

INSTITUTE FOR THE STUDY OF NONVIOLENCE JOURNAL. Bimonthly, 1969--. Institute for the Study of Nonviolence, Box 1001, Palo Alto, California 94302.

INTERCOM: A RESOURCE GUIDE AND PROGRAM CATALYST ON WAR/PEACE ISSUES. Quarterly, 1959--. Center for War/Peace Studies, 218 East 18th Street, New York, New York 10003.

INTERNATIONAL INTERACTIONS: A TRANSNATIONAL MULTI-DISCIPLINARY JOURNAL. Quarterly, 1974--. Edward E. Azar, Editor. Gordon and Breach Science Publishers, 440 Park Avenue South, New York, New York 10016.

INTERNATIONAL JOURNAL OF GROUP TENSIONS: AN INTERDISCIPLINARY QUARTERLY DEVOTED TO THE STUDY OF CONFLICT AND VIOLENCE IN HUMAN RELATIONSHIPS. Quarterly, 1971--. Journal of the International Organization for the Study of Group Tensions, Inc. Benjamin B. Wolman, Editor. Sage Publications, 275 South Beverly Drive, Beverly Hills, California 90212.

INTERNATIONAL ORGANIZATION. Quarterly, 1947--. Robert O. Keohane, Editor. Journal of the World Peace Foundation and the University of Wisconsin. Journals Department, University of Wisconsin Press, Box 1379, Madison, Wisconsin 53701.

INTERNATIONAL PEACE RESEARCH NEWSLETTER. Approximately 6 issues per year, 1963--. Publication of the International Peace Research Association. M. Rafiq Khan, Managing Editor. Gandhian Institute of Studies, P. O. Box 116, Rajghat, Varanasi-221001, India.

INTERNATIONAL PEACE STUDIES NEWSLETTER. Quarterly. Center for Peace Studies, University of Akron, Akron, Ohio 44325.

INTERNATIONAL SECURITY. Quarterly, 1976--. Program for Science and International Affairs, Harvard University, 9 Divinity Avenue, Cambridge, Massachusetts 02138.

INTERNATIONAL STUDIES QUARTERLY. Quarterly, 1957--. Journal of the International Studies Association. Sage Publications, 275 South Beverly Drive, Beverly Hills, California 90212.

JOURNAL OF ARMS CONTROL: AN APPLIED RESEARCH QUARTERLY. Quarterly, 1963--. Institute for Arms Control and Peace Research, P. O. Box 1106, Ann Arbor, Michigan 48106.

JOURNAL OF CONFLICT RESOLUTION: RESEARCH ON WAR AND PEACE BETWEEN AND WITHIN NATIONS. Quarterly, 1957--. Bruce M. Russett, Editor. Yale University, 124 Prospect Street, New Haven, Connecticut 06520. Sage Publications, 275 South Beverly Drive, Beverly Hills, California 90212.

JOURNAL OF GANDHIAN STUDIES. Quarterly, 1973--. BiNiAgthana, Editor. Indian Society of Gandhian Studies, University of Allahabad, Allahabad, India.

JOURNAL OF PEACE RESEARCH. Quarterly, 1964--. Johan Galtung, Editor. U.S. address: Universitetsforlaget, P. O. Box 142, Boston, Massachusetts 02113. Former title: JOURNAL OF PEACE.

JOURNAL OF PEACE SCIENCE: AN INTERNATIONAL JOURNAL OF THE SCIENTIFIC STUDY OF CONFLICT AND CONFLICT MANAGEMENT. Semi-annually, 1973--. Bruce D. Fitzgerald and Walter Isard, Editors. Publication of the Peace Science Division, World Friends Research Center, in collaboration with the Department of Peace Science, University of Pennsylvania and the Peace Science Society (International). Peace Science Society (International), Department of Peace Science, 3718 Locust Street, University of Pennsylvania, Philadelphia, Pennsylvania 19174.

JOURNAL OF POLITICAL AND MILITARY SOCIOLOGY: AN INTERNATIONAL AND INTERDISCIPLINARY BIANNUAL PUBLICATION. Semi-annually, 1973--. George A. Kourvetaris, Editor. Department of Sociology, Northern Illinois University, Dekalb, Illinois 60115.

JOURNAL OF THE CONFLICT RESEARCH SOCIETY. Since 1977. Richardson Institute for Conflict and Peace Research, Department of Politics, Fylde College, University of Lancaster, Bailrigg, Lancaster LA 1 4YF, England.

LATIN AMERICA AND EMPIRE REPORT. Monthly, except May-June and July-August. North American Congress on Latin America, P. O. Box 57, Cathedral Park Station, New York, New York 10025. Former title: NACLA NEWSLETTER.

NONVIOLENCE ET SOCIETE. Bimonthly. Jean van Lierde, Editor. Mouvement International de la Reconciliation et Internationale des Resistants a la Guerre. International Fellowship of Reconciliation and War Resisters' International, Rue van Elewijck 35, 1050 Brussels, Belgium.

OUR GENERATION. Quarterly, 1961--. Dimitrios Roussopoulos, Editor. 3934 rue St. Urbain, Montreal 131, Canada. Former title: OUR GENERATION AGAINST NUCLEAR WAR.

PACIFIST. Monthly, 1961--. Myrtle Solomon and Hilda Morris, Editors. Peace Pledge Union, 6 Endsleigh Street, London WC1, England.

PAX. Semi-annually, 1970--. Council for a Department of Peace, 110 Maryland Avenue N.E., Washington, D.C. 20002.

PAX ET LIBERTAS. Quarterly, 1925--. Edith Ballantyne, Editor. Women's International League for Peace and Freedom, 1 rue Varembe, 1211 Geneva 20, Switzerland. Occasional articles in French and German.

PEACE AND CHANGE: A JOURNAL OF PEACE RESEARCH. Approximately 3 issues per year, 1972--. Sponsored by the Conference on Peace Research in History. Han-shen Lin, Managing Editor. California State College, Sonoma, 1801 East Cotati Avenue, Rohnert Park, California 94928.

PEACE AND FREEDOM. 9 issues per year, 1941--. Barbara Armentrout, Editor. Women's International League for Peace and Freedom, 1213 Race Street, Philadelphia, Pennsylvania 19107. Former title: FOUR LIGHTS.

PEACE AND FREEDOM. Quarterly, 1952--. Women's International League for Peace and Freedom. B. M. Coppock, Bara Cottage, Tai Cochion, the Waew, St. Asaph Lliyoag, Clwyd LL17 OAG, N. Wales.

PEACE AND THE SCIENCES. Quarterly, 1969--. International Institute for Peace, Möllwaldplatz 5, A-1040, Vienna, Austria. In English and German.

PEACE BULLETIN. Quarterly, 1946--. Gay Hamerton, Editor. New Zealand Christian Pacifist Society, Box 2400, Wellington C.1, New Zealand. Former title: NEW ZEALAND CHRISTIAN PACIFIST.

PEACE COURRIER. Monthly, 1966--. World Peace Council, Lonnretinkatu 25 A, Helsinki 18, Finland. In English, French, German and Spanish.

PEACE MONITOR. Since 1968. British Peace Committee, 84 Claverton Street, London S.W. 1, England.

PEACE NEWS: FOR NONVIOLENT REVOLUTION. Weekly, 1936--. Peace News Limited, 5 Caledonian Road, London N1, England.

PEACE NEWSLETTER: CENTRAL NEW YORK'S ANTIWAR/SOCIAL JUSTICE PAPER. Monthly, 1936--. Syracuse Peace Council, 924 Burnet Avenue, Syracuse, New York 13203.

PEACE PRESS: AN INTERNATIONAL INFORMATION SERVICE. Monthly, 1965--. Peggy Duff, Editor. International Confederation for Disarmament and Peace, 6 Endsleigh Street, London W.C. 1, England.

PEACE RESEARCH: A QUARTERLY JOURNAL OF ORIGINAL RESEARCH ON THE PROBLEM OF WAR. Quarterly (formerly monthly), 1969--. Norman Z. Alcock, Editor. Canadian Peace Research Institute, 119 Thomas Street, Oakville L6J 3A7, Ontario, Canada.

PEACE RESEARCH ABSTRACTS JOURNAL, see BIBLIOGRAPHIES Section.

PEACE RESEARCH IN JAPAN. Japan Peace Research Group, c/o Professor Takeshi Ishida, Institute of Social Science, University of Tokyo, Hongo 7-3-1, Bunkyo-ku, Tokyo, Japan.

PEACE RESEARCH REVIEWS. Irregularly, 1967--. Alan Newcombe and Hanna Newcombe, Co-Editors. Canadian Peace Research Institute, Editorial Office, 25 Dundana Avenue, Dundas, Ontario L9H 4E5, Canada.

PEACEMAKER. Every 3 weeks, 1948--. Alice Ann Carpenter and John Leininger, Editors. Peacemaker Movement, 1255 Paddock Hills Avenue, Cincinnati, Ohio 45229.

RECONCILIACION. Bi-monthly. Carlos T. Gattinoni, Director. Movimiento de Reconciliacion en la Argentina, Rivadavia 4044, Buenos Aires, Argentina.

REPORTER FOR CONSCIENCE SAKE. Monthly, 1940--. Warren Hoover and John Wagoner, Editors. National Interreligious Service Board for Conscientious Objectors, 550 Washington Building, 15th Street and New York Avenue N.W., Washington, D.C. 20005.

SATYAGRAHA. Monthly, 1969--. Kevin M. Clark, Editor. Chicago Clergy and Laity Concerned, 542 South Dearborn Street, Chicago, Illinois 60605.

TERRORISM: AN INTERNATIONAL JOURNAL. Quarterly. Publication of the National Strategy Information Center, New York. Crane, Russak and Company, 347 Madison Avenue, New York, New York 10017.

TRANSNATIONAL ASSOCIATIONS. Monthly, 1956--. Union of International Associations, 1 rue aux Laines, 1000 Brussels, Belgium. Former title: INTERNATIONAL ASSOCIATIONS.

TRANSNATIONAL PERSPECTIVES. Quarterly, 1974--. Rene Wadlow, Editor. World Association of World Federalists, Leliegracht 21, Amsterdam-c, Netherlands.

XX CENTURY AND PEACE: BULLETIN OF THE SOVIET PEACE COMMITTEE. Monthly, 1970--. Moscow News, 16/2 Gorky Street, "Izvestia" Printshop, Moscow, USSR. In English, French, German, Russian and Spanish.

UNITAR NEWS. Quarterly, 1969--. Christina McDougal, Editor. United Nations Institute for Training and Research (UNITAR), 801 United Nations Plaza, New York, New York 10017. Separate English and French editions.

VISTA OF THE UNA: MAGAZINE OF THE UNITED NATIONS ASSOCIATION OF THE U.S.A. Bimonthly, 1965--. Albert H. Fransworth, Editor. UNA--USA, 345 East 46th Street, New York, New York 10017.

W R I NEWSLETTER. Monthly. Heinz Werner Engel, Editor. War Resisters International, Van Elewyckstraat 35, 1050 Brussels, Belgium.

W R L NEWS. Bi-monthly, 1948--. Jim Peck, Editor. War Resisters League, 339 Lafayette Street, New York, New York 10012.

WAR/PEACE REPORT. Monthly (10 issues per year, 1967-1975), 1961-1975. Center for War/Peace Studies, 218 East 18th Street, New York, New York 10003.

WAR RESISTANCE. Quarterly, 1934--. Heinz Werner Engel, Editor. War Resisters' International, Van Elewyckstraat 35, 1050 Brussels, Belgium. In English, French and German. Former title: WAR RESISTER.

WIN: PEACE AND FREEDOM THRU NONVIOLENT ACTION. Weekly, 1965--. War Resisters League, 339 Lafayette Street, New York, New York 10001.

WOMEN STRIKE FOR PEACE. Quarterly, 1962--. Jean Shulman, Editor. Women Strike for Peace, 799 Broadway, New York, New York 10003.

WORLD AFFAIRS. Quarterly (except 1878-1884), 1834--. Cornelius W. Vable, Jr., Managing Editor. American Peace Society, Room 304, 4000 Albemarle Street N.W., Washington, D.C. 20016. Former title: ADVOCATE OF PEACE.

WORLD AFFAIRS DIGEST, see BIBLIOGRAPHIES Section.

WORLD CITIZEN/FEDERALIST LETTER. Monthly (10 issues per year), 1947--. World Federalists, USA, 1424 16th Street N.W., Washington, D.C. 20036.

WORLD FEDERATION. Monthly, 1929--. Shiva Kumar, Editor. P.M.V. Keshighat, Vrindaban, Uttar Pradesh, India.

WORLD PEACE. Quarterly. International Society of United Modern Enterprise, 60a, Campbell Street, P. O. Box 1944, Lagos, Nigeria.

WORLD PEACE NEWS. 9 issues per year, 1970--. Thomas Liggett, Editor. American Movement for World Government, Inc., 777 United Nations Plaza, New York, New York 10017.

WORLD POLITICS: A QUARTERLY JOURNAL OF INTERNATIONAL RELATIONS. Quarter, 1948--. Klaus Knorr, Editor. Princeton University Press, Box 231, Princeton, New Jersey 08540.

YALE STUDIES IN WORLD PUBLIC ORDER. Semi-annually. Eisuke Suzuki, Editor. Box 2102, Yale Station, New Haven, Connecticut 06520.

Bibliographies

Aggarwal, Lalit K. "Peace Science: A Bibliography." Philadelphia: Department of Peace Science, University of Pennsylvania, 1974. Mimeo.

Alexander, Yonah. "Selected Bibliography," in Yonah Alexander, Editor, INTERNATIONAL TERRORISM: NATIONAL, REGIONAL AND GLOBAL PERSPECTIVES. New York: Praeger, 1976.

Allen, Patricia R. B., and Albert J. Rutledge. "An Annotated Bibliography of Mostly Obscure Articles on Human Territorial Behavior." Monticello, Ill.: Council of Planning Librarians, 1975.

Angell, Robert C. "The Sociology of International Relations: A Trend Report and Bibliography." CURRENT SOCIOLOGY, 14, 1 (1966), 5-62.

ARMS CONTROL AND DISARMAMENT: A QUARTERLY BIBLIOGRAPHY WITH ABSTRACTS AND ANNOTATIONS. Edited by U.S. Arms Control and Disarmament Agency. Washington, D.C.: U.S. Government Printing Office, Winter 1964-65 to Spring 1973.

Atherton, Alexine L. INTERNATIONAL ORGANIZATIONS: A GUIDE TO INFORMATION SOURCES. Detroit: Gale Research Company, 1976.

Baringer, Richard E., and Robert K. Ramers. "Bibliography," in Richard E. Barringer and Robert K. Ramers, WAR: PATTERNS OF CONFLICT. Cambridge, Mass.: MIT Press, 1972.

Beitz, Charles R., A. Michael Washburn, and Thomas G. Weiss, Editors. PEACE STUDIES: COLLEGE COURSES ON PEACE AND WORLD ORDER. New York: Institute for World Order, 1973.

Bienen, Henry. VIOLENCE AND SOCIAL CHANGE: A REVIEW OF CURRENT LITERATURE. Chicago: University of Chicago Press, for the Adlai Stevenson Institute of International Affairs, 1968.

Blackey, Robert. MODERN RESOLUTIONS AND REVOLUTIONS: A BIBLIOGRAPHY. Santa Barbara, Calif.: American Bibliographical Center-Clio, 1976.

Blumberg, Herbert. "Annotated Bibliography of Serials Concerned With the Non-violent Protest Movement." SOCIOLOGICAL ABSTRACTS, 17 4 (1969), xxi-xxxvi; and 17, 5 (1969), xxxix-xxx.

Bramson, Leon, and George W. Goethals. "Selected Bibliography," in Leon Bramson and George W. Goethals, Editors, WAR: STUDIES FROM PSYCHOLOGY, SOCIOLOGY, ANTHROPOLOGY. Revised Edition. New York: Basic Books, 1968.

Brown, Laura Ferris. A SELECTED BIBLIOGRAPHY OF INTERNATIONAL ARBITRATION 1970-1976. New York: Eastman Library of the American Arbitration Association, 1976.

Burns, Richard Dean. ARMS CONTROL AND DISARMAMENT: A BIBLIOGRAPHY. Santa Barbara, Calif.: American Bibliographical Center-Clio, 1977.

Burt, Richard. CONGRESSIONAL HEARINGS ON AMERICAN DEFENSE POLICY, 1947-1971: AN ANNOTATED BIBLIOGRAPHY. Lawrence: University of Kansas, for the National Security Education Program of New York University, 1974.

Caplow, Theodore. "Bibliography on Coalitions in Triads," in TWO AGAINST ONE. Englewood Cliffs, N.J.: Prentice-Hall, 1968.

Carter, April, David Hoggett, and Adam Roberts. NON-VIOLENT ACTION, THEORY AND PRACTICE: A SELECTED BIBLIOGRAPHY. Haverford, Pa.: Center for Nonviolent Conflict Resolution, Haverford College, 1970.

Center for the Study of Armament and Disarmament. POLITICAL ISSUES BIBLIOGRAPHY SERIES. Irregularly, 1972--. Susan Hoffman, Editor. Center for the Study of Armament and Disarmament, California State University, Los Angeles, 5151 State University Drive, Los Angeles, California 90032.

Center for War/Peace Studies. CONFLICT: A GUIDE TO SELECTED CURRICULUM MATERIALS. New York: Center for War/Peace Studies, 1973.

Center for War/Peace Studies. CURRICULUM MATERIALS ON WAR, PEACE, CONFLICT AND CHANGE: AN ANNOTATED BIBLIOGRAPHY, with a list of Organizational Resources. New York: Center for War/Peace Studies, 1972.

Clark, Ignatius Frederick. "Bibliography," in VOICES PROPHESYING WAR: 1763-1984. London: Oxford University Press, 1966.

Communications Institute. DIRECTORY OF PEACE AND CONFLICT PROGRAMMES. New York: Communications Institute, Academy for Educational Development, 1974.

Cook, Blanche Wiesen. BIBLIOGRAPHY ON PEACE RESEARCH IN HISTORY. Santa Barbara, Calif.: American Bibliographical Center-Clio, 1969.

Crawford, Elizabeth T. THE SOCIAL SCIENCES IN INTERNATIONAL AND MILITARY POLICY: AN ANALYTIC BIBLIOGRAPHY. Washington, D.C.: Bureau of Social Science Research, 1965.

de Grazia, Alfred, Editor. THE UNIVERSAL REFERENCE SYSTEM, POLITICAL SCIENCE, GOVERNMENT. Princeton, N.J.: Princeton Research Publishing Company, 1969.

Denisoff, R. Serge. SONGS OF PROTEST: WAR AND PEACE--A BIBLIOGRAPHY AND DISCOGRAPHY. Santa Barbara, Calif.: American Bibliographical Center-Clio, 1973.

DeVore, Ronald M. THE ARAB-ISRAELI CONFLICT: A HISTORICAL, POLITICAL, SOCIAL AND MILITARY BIBLIOGRAPHY. Santa Barbara, Calif.: American Bibliographical Center-Clio, 1976.

Dexter, Byron Vinson, assisted by Elizabeth H. Bryant, and Janice L. Murray. THE FOREIGN AFFAIRS 50-YEAR BIBLIOGRAPHY: NEW EVALUATION OF SIGNIFICANT BOOKS ON INTERNATIONAL RELATIONS: 1920-1970. New York: Bowker, for the Council on Foreign Relations, 1972.

Divale, William Tulio. WARFARE IN PRIMITIVE SOCIETIES: A BIBLIOGRAPHY. Santa Barbara, Calif.: American Bibliographical Center-Clio, 1973.

Dougall, Lucy. THE WAR PEACE FILM GUIDE. Revised Edition. Chicago: World Without War Publications, 1973.

Dunn, John. "Bibliography: A Guide to Further Readings," in John Dunn, Editor, MODERN REVOLUTIONS: AN INTRODUCTION TO THE ANALYSIS OF A POLITICAL PHENOMENON. New York: Cambridge University Press, 1972.

Foreign Policy Association. "Bibliography on Simulation." SOCIAL EDUCATION, 33 (February 1969), 195-199.

Gibbs, G. I., Editor. HANDBOOK OF GAMES AND SIMULATION EXERCISES. Beverly Hills, Calif.: Sage, 1974.

Ginsberg, Robert. "A Bibliography of the Philosophy of War in the Atomic Age," in Robert Ginsberg, Editor, THE CRITIQUE OF WAR: CONTEMPORARY PHILOSOPHICAL EXPLORATIONS. Chicago: Henry Regnery, 1969.

Grech, Anthony P. "Selected Bibliography on the Middle East Crisis," in Quincy Wright, Editor, THE MIDDLE EAST: PROSPECTS FOR PEACE, BACKGROUND PAPERS AND PROCEEDINGS OF THE THIRTEENTH HAMMARSKJOLD FORUM. Dobbs Ferry, N.Y.: Oceana, for the Association of the Bar of the City of New York, 1969.

Greenwood, John. AMERICAN DEFENSE POLICY SINCE 1945: A PRELIMINARY BIBLIOGRAPHY. Lawrence: University Press of Kansas, 1973.

Gurr, Ted Robert. "A Historical and Comparative Bibliography of Group Conflict and Violence," in Hugh Davis Graham and Ted Robert Gurr, Editors, VIOLENCE IN AMERICA: HISTORICAL AND COMPARATIVE PERSPECTIVES. Revised Edition. New York: Bantam Books, 1970.

Haas, Michael. INTERNATIONAL ORGANIZATIONS AND INSTITUTIONS BIBLIOGRAPHY. Stanford, Calif.: Hoover Institution Press, 1971.

Hennen, Thomas J., Jr., and Vida C. Stanton. "Let There Be Peace: An Annotated Bibliography of Anti-War Literature and Realistic Fiction about War." LANGUAGE ARTS, 54, 1 (January 1977).

Hernes, Helga. THE MULTINATIONAL CORPORATION: A GUIDE TO INFORMATION SOURCES. Detroit: Gale Research Company, 1977.

Howard, Harry N. THE MIDDLE EAST: A SELECTED BIBLIOGRAPHY OF RECENT WORKS, 1960-70. Washington, D.C.: The Middle East Institute, 1970.

Hyatt, John. PACIFISM: A SELECTED BIBLIOGRAPHY. London: Housmans, 1972.

International Organizations. "Selected Bibliography." INTERNATIONAL ORGANIZATIONS, 28, 2 (Spring 1974), 297-311.

International Peace Research Institute, Oslo. "List of Publications." JOURNAL OF PEACE RESEARCH, 7, 2 (1970), 175-184.

International Sociological Association. "An Annotated Bibliography," in THE NATURE OF CONFLICT, STUDIES ON THE SOCIOLOGICAL ASPECTS OF INTERNATIONAL TENSIONS. Paris: United Nations Educational, Scientific, and Cultural Organization, 1957.

Jacobsen, Kurt, Christien Boe Kielland, and Knut Myklebust. REPRESENTATION AT THE UNITED NATIONS: A STATISTICAL HANDBOOK. Oslo: International Peace Research Institute, 1973.

Jones, Susan D., and J. David Singer. BEYOND CONJECTURE IN INTERNATIONAL POLITICS: ABSTRACTS OF DATA-BASED RESEARCH. Itasca, Ill.: Peacock, 1972.

JOURNAL OF PEACE RESEARCH. "Book Notes." Annotated listings of recent books published in each issue.

Judge, Anthony J. N., and Kjell Skjelsbaek. BIBLIOGRAPHY OF DOCUMENTS ON TRANSNATIONAL ASSOCIATIONS NETWORKS: INTERNATIONAL NON-GOVERNMENTAL ORGANIZATION AS A FIELD OF STUDY. Brussels: Union of International Associations, 1972.

Kelleher, Catherine M. "Bibliography on Political-Military Systems," in Catherine M. Kelleher, Editor, POLITICAL-MILITARY SYSTEMS: COMPARATIVE PERSPECTIVES. Beverly Hills, Calif.: Sage, 1974.

Keohane, Robert O., and Joseph S. Nye, Jr. "Selected Bibliography," in Robert O. Keohane and Josephy S. Nye, Jr., Editors, TRANSNATIONAL RELATIONS AND WORLD POLITICS. Cambridge, Mass.: Harvard University Press, 1971.

Kresling, Janis A. FOREIGN AFFAIRS BIBLIOGRAPHY. New York: Bowker, 1976.

Kresling, Janis A., et al., Editors. "Recent Books on International Relations." Annotated listings in each issue of FOREIGN AFFAIRS.

LaBarr, Dorothy F., and J. David Singer. THE STUDY OF INTERNATIONAL POLITICS: A GUIDE TO THE SOURCES FOR THE STUDENT, TEACHER, AND RESEARCHER. Santa Barbara, Calif.: American Bibliographical Center-Clio, 1976.

Lang, Kurt. MILITARY INSTITUTIONS AND THE SOCIOLOGY OF WAR: A REVIEW OF THE LITERATURE WITH ANNOTATED BIBLIOGRAPHY. Beverly Hills, Calif.: Sage, 1971.

Larson, Arthur D. CIVIL-MILITARY RELATIONS AND MILITARISM: A CLASSIFIED BIBLIOGRAPHY COVERING THE UNITED STATES AND OTHER NATIONS OF THE WORLD WITH INTRODUCTORY NOTES. Manhattan: Kansas State University Library, 1971.

Legault, Albert. PEACE-KEEPING OPERATIONS: BIBLIOGRAPHY. Paris: International Information Center on Peace-Keeping Operations, 1967.

Leitenberg, Milton, and Richard Dean Burns. THE VIETNAM CONFLICT: ITS DIMENSIONS, POLITICAL TRAUMAS, AND MILITARY DEVELOPMENTS. Santa Barbara, Calif.: American Bibliographical Center-Clio, 1973.

Little, Roger W. "General Bibliography," and "Bibliography the Inter-University Seminar on Armed Forces and Society," in Roger W. Little, Editor, HANDBOOK OF MILITARY INSTITUTIONS. Beverly Hills, Calif.: Sage, 1971.

McGowan, Patrick J., and Howard B. Shapiro. THE COMPARATIVE STUDY OF FOREIGN POLICY: A SURVEY OF SCIENTIFIC FINDINGS. Beverly Hills, Calif.: Sage, 1973.

Manheim, Jarol B., and Melanie Wallace. POLITICAL VIOLENCE IN THE UNITED STATES, 1875-1974: A BIBLIOGRAPHY. New York: Garland, 1975.

Middle East Research and Information Project. "MERIP Reading Guide." MERIP REPORTS, 28 (May 1974), 11-22.

Miller, Albert Jay. CONFRONTATION, CONFLICT, AND DISSENT: A BIBLIOGRAPHY OF A DECADE OF CONTROVERSY, 1960-1970. Metuchen, N.J.: Scarecrow Press, 1972.

Nesbitt, William A. "Simulation Games and a Global Perspective," and "Finding Out More." INTERCOM (Issue on Teaching Global Issues Through Simulation), 75 (Summer 1974), 24-32.

Nesbitt, William A., Editor. TEACHING ABOUT WAR AND ITS CONTROL: A SELECTIVE ANNOTATED BIBLIOGRAPHY FOR THE SOCIAL STUDIES TEACHER. Albany: University of the State of New York, 1972.

Newcombe, Hanna, and Alan Newcombe. "References," in PEACE RESEARCH AROUND THE WORLD. Oakville, Ontario: Canadian Peace Research Institute, 1969.

PEACE RESEARCH ABSTRACTS JOURNAL. Alan Newcombe and Hanna Newcombe, Editors. Oakville, Ontario: Canadian Peace Research Institute. Monthly, June 1964--.

Pickus, Robert, and Robert Woito. TO END WAR--AN INTRODUCTION: IDEAS, BOOKS, ORGANIZATIONS, WORK THAT CAN HELP. Revised Edition. New York: Harper and Row, for the World Without War Council, 1970.

Rai, Hira. BIBLIOGRAPHY ON NONVIOLENCE AND SATY-AGRAHA. Introduction by Sugata Dasgupta. Rajghat, Varanasi, India: Navachetna Prakashan, for the Gandhian Institute of Studies, 1971.

Rosenberg, Douglas H., and Major Raoul H. Alcalá, U.S. Army. "The New Politics of National Security: A Selected and Annotated Research Bibliography," in Bruce M. Russett and Alfred Stepan, Editors, MILITARY FORCE AND AMERICAN SOCIETY. New York: Harper and Row, 1973.

Roswell, Judith. ARMS CONTROL, DISARMAMENT, AND ECONOMIC PLANNING: A LIST OF SOURCES. Santa Barbara, Calif.: American Bibliographical Center-Clio, 1973.

Sariola, Sakari, Sandra Binns, and Caroline Karlin, Compilers; and Janet P. Barber, Editor. "War and Peace: An Annotated Bibliography." KANSAS JOURNAL OF SOCIOLOGY, 7, 3 and 4 (Fall/Winter 1971), 148-165.

Scharffenorth, G., and W. Huber. BIBLIOGRAPHIC ZUR FRIEDENSFORSCHUNG. Stuttgart, Germany: E. Klett, 1970.

Senghaas, Dieter. "Bibliography: Recent Peace Research Books in the Federal Republic of Germany by German Authors." JOURNAL OF PEACE RESEARCH, 10, 3 (1973), 317-318.

Sharpe, Summer M., and Rick Paulson. SOME PERSPEC-TIVES ON CONFLICT: A SELECTED BIBLIOGRAPHY. Monticello, Ill.: Council of Planning Librarians, 1974.

Sica, Geraldine P. "A Preliminary Bibliography of Studies of the Economic Effects of Defense Policies and Expenditures," in Seymour Melman, Editor, THE DEFENSE ECONOMY. New York: Praeger, 1970.

Spurgin, John H., and Gary R. Smith. GLOBAL DIMENSIONS IN THE NEW SOCIAL STUDIES. Boulder, Colo.: Educational Resources Information Center/ Clearinghouse for Social Studies/Social Science Education (ERIC/Chess), 1973.

Strharsky, Harry, and Mary Riesch, with Bill Arnnold, and Colleen O'Connor, Editors. BIBLIOGRAPHICAL NOTES FOR UNDERSTANDING THE TRANSNATIONAL CORPORATIONS AND THE THIRD WORLD. Washington, D.C.: CoDoC International Secretariat, 1975.

Student Forum on International Order and World Peace. STUDIES TOWARD PEACE: A COMPENDIUM OF SELECTED UNDERGRADUATE AND GRADUATE COURSES IN 'PEACE AND WORLD ORDER.' 2 Volumes. New York: Student Forum on International Order and World Peace, 1969.

United Nations Educational, Scientific, and Cultural Organization. INTERNATIONAL REPERTORY OF INSTITUTIONS FOR PEACE AND CONFLICT RESEARCH. Paris: United Nations Educational, Scientific, and Cultural Organization, 1973.

United Nations Educational, Scientific, and Cultural Organization. REVIEW OF RESEARCH TRENDS AND AN ANNOTATED BIBLIOGRAPHY: SOCIAL AND ECONOMIC CONSEQUENCES OF THE ARMS RACE AND OF DISARMAMENT. Paris: United Nations Educational, Scientific, and Cultural Organization, 1978.

Vir, Dharma. GANDHI BIBLIOGRAPHY. Chandigarh, Punjab, Haryana, and Himachal Pradesh. India: Gandhi Smarak Nidhi, 1967.

Weston, Burns H., Sherle R. Schwenninger, and Diane E. Shamis. PEACE AND WORLD ORDER STUDIES: A CURRICULUM GUIDE. New York: Transnational Academic Program, Institute for World Order, 1978.

Winter, J. M. "Selected Bibliography of Works on War and Economic Development," in J. M. Winter, Editor, WAR AND ECONOMIC DEVELOPMENT: ESSAYS IN MEMORY OF DAVID JOSLIN. New York: Cambridge University Press, 1975.

WORLD AFFAIRS DIGEST: CURRENT THOUGHTS ON PEACE AND WAR. L. Larry Leonard, Editor. Department of Political Science, Wisconsin State University, Oshkosh, Wisconsin 54901. Irregularly published.

Wright, Quincy. "Select Bibliography on War, 1945-64." Appendix H to "Commentary on War Since 1942," in Quincy Wright, Editor, A STUDY OF WAR. Chicago: University of Chicago Press, 1965.